IT's ALL about the PEOPLE

Technology Management That Overcomes Disaffected People, Stupid Processes, and Deranged Corporate Cultures

IT's ALL about the PEOPLE

Technology Management That Overcomes Disaffected People, Stupid Processes, and Deranged Corporate Cultures

STEPHEN J. ANDRIOLE

CRC Press
Taylor & Francis Group
Boca Raton   London   New York

CRC Press is an imprint of the
Taylor & Francis Group, an **informa** business
AN AUERBACH BOOK

CRC Press
Taylor & Francis Group
6000 Broken Sound Parkway NW, Suite 300
Boca Raton, FL 33487-2742

© 2012 by Taylor & Francis Group, LLC
CRC Press is an imprint of Taylor & Francis Group, an Informa business

No claim to original U.S. Government works

Printed in the United States of America on acid-free paper
Version Date: 2011909

International Standard Book Number: 978-1-4398-7658-9 (Hardback)

Visit the Taylor & Francis Web site at
http://www.taylorandfrancis.com

and the CRC Press Web site at
http://www.crcpress.com

Contents

Preface

If you're new to technology management, then much of what appears in this book will strike you as opinionated, cynical, and arrogant. But if you've been at IT for a while now, you'll see the contents as accumulated wisdom. I've written the book for those who have been in the trenches for a long time and for those who want to skip right to the advanced course in gonzo technology management, skipping the pleasantries of undergraduate interning at your average consulting company or within the discontented ranks of your typical struggling company.

The assumption here is that the business technology relationship can be widened and deepened to yield significant business value. But there are landmines everywhere. Many of the explosions that result are self-inflicted, almost deliberate, because we seem almost incapable of fixing the same old problems with people, processes, organizations, and corporate cultures, not technology, which by and large works well.

Technology management is challenging. IT's a moving target, at best. The technologies themselves keep changing and the role we expect them to play keeps evolving. The nuances of managing in such a fluid environment are multidimensional: it's about the biases of management, vendor manipulation, and ambiguous project requirements, and lots more insidious nefarious realities.

There's a need to cut right to the chase. We seem to take two steps forward and one backward year after year, project after project, and now there's unprecedented budget pressure to reduce costs, reduce costs, and, in addition, reduce costs. I'm personally frustrated by our inability to routinely integrate acquisition, deployment, and support best practices in our technology management routines. How many toes must one shoot off before it's impossible to walk?

But I also realize—after decades in this business—that, by and large, cost-effective technology management is much more about people, personal relationships, and corporate culture than it is about the technology itself or management "best practices." In fact, I could argue that technology and the processes we use to optimize IT are really pretty meaningless unless you're surrounded by the right people allowed to do the right things. Put another way, IT doesn't work if you're surrounded by bad people and stupid processes immersed in a deranged corporate culture.

Everyone knows this. We just choose (because we're bad, stupid, and deranged) not to talk about it. We prefer talking about servers, desktops, operating systems, BI, CRM, ERP, and anything else that distracts us from what really moves technology management: the human factor. The digital stuff is easy; the organic stuff is hard.

There's no conflict avoidance here. I hope I've blended realistic best practices with the best and worst of the human species. I've also acknowledged the huge impact that corporate cultures and the knowledge, skills, personalities, and experience of the senior management team have on how well or badly we do IT. We all know that the talent of the SMT varies widely from company to company: we hate telling undergraduates that many CEOs are idiots and that they got their positions not because of their performance but because of their personal relationships, because of who they knew, not what they know or did. But you already knew this.

The book opens with a look at the people who surround the technology management process. We have to start there. The insights about people presented in Chapter 1 include the best and worst of human behavior and the best and worst about managers, executives, and corporate cultures. But let me warn you now: the insights are mostly bad. Not that "bad" paralyzes us. There are lots of ways to neutralize "bad" and even get to "good." ("Great" is really elusive.)

Chapter 2 is about organizational politics, among other reporting, governance, and power realities. The twenty-first century is sending clear messages about how to acquire, deploy, and support technology through new organizational structures and processes. Total control will yield to shared control. Standardization will be situational. Operational technology will divorce from strategic technology. Are you listening? Chapter 2 describes the trends that will change your world. You need to prepare for these changes and, if your leadership and culture permit (or can be manipulated), lead your companies' organizational change initiatives. It's really simple: change or fail.

Chapter 3 looks at new management best practices, given the perennial constraints of people, processes, and cultures. It talks about the management strategies and tactics that make sense today, and for the foreseeable future (as well as the ones that make no sense at all). It challenges the traditional with the progressive. Sound familiar? What should the new TCO and ROI look like? What works and what doesn't? Read closely. There's lots to do.

Chapter 4 explores sourcing. Not very much new here, except the whole God-damned chapter. Outsourcing is heading to the cloud. Don't believe me? Look around. You're already in the cloud but probably don't talk about "cloud computing." X-as-a-service is at your service. It's the future. Get used to it. Better yet, exploit it. What the hell are you waiting for? Oh, I forgot, you just love hosting monster software applications and paying huge annual maintenance fees. The new technology delivery models represent the greatest opportunity to save money and make money with technology that we've seen in decades.

A conclusion suggests what you might want to do tomorrow, or whenever you finish reading this book. It starts with the new basics, which are really the old basics seen through a twenty-first-century lens.

All of this is about transformation and success. Our clients have mastered the soft art of people/process/organization/culture manipulation and exploitation, while buying, deploying, and supporting the right technology. But they've long since accepted the human factor as the major driver of success. Everyone can improve technology's ability to save money and make money for the business if they acknowledge the major role that people, processes, organizations, and culture play in the process. We have seen tremendous success with companies that focus more on these variables than on technology itself.

When you've completed this journey I hope you'll be angry enough and more than ready for some change. But that depends on you. If the U.S. federal government's Troubled Asset Relief Program (TARP), the wars in Iraq and Afghanistan, the healthcare debacle, and the cozy financial relationship among business, lobbyists, and your elected officials don't get you angry, then this book is unlikely to move you. But if you've had enough, then maybe you're ready to join the ranks of our clients who have optimized their investments in business technology by focusing on organic, not digital, opportunities.

A final word. Dealing with people, processes, organizations, and corporate cultures is far more difficult than configuring servers, updating desktops, or tracking service-level agreements. They are the elephants in the room. If you focus on them more than on the technology itself, you can dramatically improve service and agility. If you fail you will fight one war after another and never have a calm day at the office. Sophisticated executives and managers know this. The determined ones get IT done.

1

People

This chapter looks at all of the people in our professional lives. (You can assess the ones in your personal life.)

Do we have to?

Yes, I'm afraid we do, because when all's said and done, getting anything right depends on the people in our lives: smart people, stupid people, and nasty people, among other descriptors we might use. Worse, all of these people exist in insane asylums we call teams, organizations, and corporations. OK, I've offended you already. But you tell me, how many organizations are sane and improve the mental health of the inmates?

We're stuck with people, people, and more people, many of whom have no idea what they're doing or have long since stopped caring about what they do—or—OMG—both. Of course, there are solid professionals out there, but many of them have been beaten down by deranged corporate cultures, clueless managers, and executives who, like heat-seeking missiles, chase ever-increasing salaries, bonuses, and stock options, in no particular order and with a particular sense of "right" or "appropriate." Don't believe me? Look at what the CIOs (chief information officers) make at Fortune 500 companies for consolidating data centers, optimizing server utilization, and standardizing desktops. Could you do these things, with huge teams and equally huge budgets, for $5,000,000 a year? Look at what investment professionals make for moving money from one global location to another. Goldman-Sachs distributed nearly $18,000,000,000 in personal bonuses in 2009 alone. Look at what talk radio hosts make. Regardless of whether you hate or love Russ Limbaugh, do you think he's worth over $400,000,000 for what he does every day? Yeah, it's about money (and, of course, some power and sex). So let's not kid ourselves about motivation or the huge role that competence and integrity play in corporate failure, or the role that greed and politics play in management decision making.

Technology management is no different. There are pretty standard unwritten protocols that explain who works hard, who loses, and who makes the most money. How well do you understand these protocols? How well do you practice them? Did you even know that they exist? (For the record, there's no relationship between what human resources [HR] tells you the path to success in your company is and the reality of following the path, which itself is usually misleading and sometimes outright deceptive. Does HR know anything?)

Let's start with some dirty little secrets. Then we'll move to other harsh realities packaged in some rants. Your job is to extract what I'm complaining about here and apply it to your world, unless, of course, you're one of the targets of the rants. In that case, your job is to run and hide if you have any shame at all. But let's make no mistake about the purpose of this book: it's to identify the sense and non-sense that surrounds business technology management and help you determine how to maneuver through the minefields that pretty much define life in the management trenches in the early twenty-first century. We end with an action plan.

SOME DIRTY LITTLE SECRETS

In the world in which we live—a world that changes almost daily—there are truths and untruths. There's hype and there's reality. There are technologies that work and there are technologies that stay forever in what the Gartner Group describes as the "trough of disillusionment." There are subtleties and nuances. There are smart people and nasty people. There are crazy organizations and there are insane corporate cultures. Let's look at some of the perceptual anomalies of your world or, if you prefer, some dirty little (and not-so-little) secrets about the people and processes in your worlds. The by-no-means exhaustive list includes:

- Many technologists are not technical; they just act like they are.
- No one knows what the hell "architecture" is.
- Technology is operational, not strategic, in spite of what they tell you at vendor conferences.
- Vendor management is an oxymoron because no one does it well.
- Software costs way too much—*way too much*—for what you get and must suffer through.

Many Technologists Are Not Technical

Many technologists, especially senior technology managers and (especially) executives, are not at all technical. This means that many of them know just enough to ask some really good questions and make some really bad decisions. There are many technology professionals who know one area really well and absolutely nothing about anything else. In my consulting practice I do a lot of executive education and technology awareness training. What I've found over the years is that there are lots of professionals who are almost completely unaware of emerging technologies or especially new technology delivery models. This is the natural result of keeping one's head down for a prolonged period of time on one task. When you finally lift up your head you realize the world has changed. Web 2.0? Mashups? Location-aware applications? The app store? SOA? EDA? The semantic web? What's going on out there?

Senior technology managers often know very little about technology. Some argue that relative ignorance is OK as long as the basics are reasonably well understood and that they have people reporting to them who really understand the technology to be acquired, deployed, and supported. Others argue that knowledge of technology management best practices is more important than understanding the bits, bytes, and lights of specific technologies. Both of these are pretty good arguments but there are some real dangers connected with technology ignorance.

First, there's a credibility issue. Technologists who spend a lot of time staying current resent, and disrespect, the lack of effort senior technology managers spend to understand technologies and technology trends. Next, vendor radar is really sensitive to shallow technology knowledge. Once a vendor profiles a client as shallow, they will exploit the ignorance to their advantage. Finally, and most important, nontechnology technologists cannot strategize. As we discuss in more detail in the architecture section below, it's difficult if not impossible to think strategically about enterprise, applications, communications, information, or security architecture if you're not technical. Service-oriented and event-driven architectures are complicated and require an understanding of integration and interoperability technology, web services, and the exploding world of open-source APIs, among other technologies. As an example of the importance of architecture, how can decisions be made regarding application development, software-as-a-service or other X-as-a-service models without an understanding of architecture? How can one make decisions about thin clients or open-source software unless these opportunities are understood in a larger architectural context?

The dirty little secret? Too many technology managers get their technology information at cocktail parties, from vendors, and from what a small number of colleagues may, or may not, tell them. Put another way, they are not "students," as we all should be in a field that annually reinvents itself. Good managers should rely upon their lieutenants; however, they should also understand the technology foundations of their investment decisions, especially all of those that involve strategic investment planning. It's tough to develop a vision in a vacuum.

No One Knows What the Hell "Architecture" Is

No one really understands "architecture." It's broad, complicated, narrow, and simple. It comes in different flavors. Vendors and consultants have vested interests in making it all sound ominous. In truth, architecture can mean different things to different people solving different problems.

Wikipedia tells us that enterprise architecture has the following practice areas:

- Business:
    - Strategy maps, goals, corporate policies, operating model
    - Functional decompositions (e.g., IDEF0, SADT), capabilities, and organizational models
    - Business processes
    - Organization cycles, periods, and timing
    - Suppliers of hardware, software, and services
- Information:
    - Metadata: data that describe your enterprise data elements
    - Data models: conceptual, logical, and physical
- Applications:
    - Application software inventories and diagrams
    - Interfaces between applications, that is, events, messages, and data flows
    - Intranet, extranet, Internet, eCommerce, EDI links with parties within and outside the organization
- Technology:
    - Hardware, platforms, and hosting: servers, and where they are kept
    - Local and wide area networks, Internet connectivity diagrams

- Operating systems
- Infrastructure software: application servers, DBMS
- Programming languages, and so on

How many of your colleagues know a lot about most of these practice areas? How many can cover them all? How about service-oriented and event-driven architectures? Communications architecture? Applications architecture?

The dirty little secret? We can say the word, but really don't understand architecture. In my travels I have actually come across companies that willingly default their understanding of—and investments in—architecture to their vendors! No kidding: SAP, IBM, and Microsoft have much more influence on the adoption of, for example, SOA and EDA than their clients.

Technology Is Operational, Not Strategic—at Least for Now

I've beaten the strategic technology drum for a long, long time. Strategic technology (you know, the stuff that touches customers and suppliers) is focused on revenue generation, improved customer service, pricing, upselling, cross-selling, and similar activities designed to contribute to profitable growth. Operational technology is about devices, networks, storage, security, disaster recovery, and other infrastructure technologies. So, where does the money go? Operational technology by a long shot. We may talk a good game about strategic technology but the fact is that there are precious few strategic technology projects, or strategic technology investors, on the planet. We scream and yell about strategic technology but we spend just about all of the money on operational technology. In adverse economic times we spend even less on strategic technology than we did the previous year and the year before that.

The dirty little secret? We talk the talk but don't walk the walk: hardly anyone has a serious strategic technology investment strategy or a portfolio of strategic technology projects that consumes more than 10% of the technology budget. Even "discretionary projects" are operational. So don't buy the hype about how strategic technology is (as sad as it is). Strategic technology is often operational technology in disguise.

Vendor Management Is an Oxymoron: No One Does it Well

Vendors usually dress better than their clients, drive nicer cars, and are often even smarter than the people who give them huge piles of money year after year. We talk a good game about kicking our vendors' asses, but they usually get the best of us. I recently discussed a major enterprise application deployment project with the managers of what turned out to be a five-year/$500,000,000 project. They used a consultancy to help them get the application installed (which got most of the money) but complained that they were assigned "kids" to work on the project, kids who received incredibly valuable on-the-job training on their nickel. The performance metrics for the project were as soft as they were hard. A *key person* clause here, a *quantitative metric* there would have gone a long way toward avoiding these kinds of problems. The $500,000,000 should have been $300,000,000. $300,000,000. What am I missing?

Most companies don't squeeze their vendors tightly enough. Nor do they partner with them enough. Instead they live in this Neverland between partnership and paranoia. The same people who just installed your network may be the same people who negotiated your help desk contract. Corporate IT finance is hardly ever experienced enough to get the most out of their vendors. They talk tough, but they're almost never formally trained in RFP or SLA development and management, contract negotiations, TCO, or ROI, among many other related areas.

The dirty little secret? On a scale of one to ten (where one is weak and ten is strong), our vendor management skills are a solid three. We think we're good at this, but we're really not very good at all. Actually, nearly all of us suck at vendor management. How good are you? Really?

Software Costs *Way* Too Much (*Way, Way Too Much*)

I don't know about you but when I have to pay $250 for Microsoft Office and $350 for the personal computer on which it runs, I get angry. What does SAP's ERP application or Oracle DBMS and their ERP suite cost? All in? The cost of enterprise software is staggering. Five-year/$500,000,000 enterprise software projects are not that unusual among the Fortune 100: $500,000,000 million dollars in five years, or about $250,000 *a day*.

Exchange servers are way out of line, especially when I can manage my e-mail with Google or Yahoo for free (or nearly free). They don't scale? Try them sometime. How about the functional spread between MySQL and SQL Server? Maintenance fees are beyond comprehension. $5,000,000 a year *for what*? Just to keep the lights on?

In a previous life I spent nearly $25,000,000 a year on software. Pretty hard to believe but it's not unusual for companies to pay hefty acquisition and maintenance fees for software they barely use, or use unproductively. Shelfware is one of the dirty little secrets of enterprise software.

Think about the Nike shirts I buy on eBay for $20 that cost $50 to $75 in retail stores (that I have yet to physically visit). Or the pet food I buy at Costco for 40% less than the grocery store. Or the luggage I buy at Overstock.com, the same luggage that's 100% more at the department store at the mall. Why isn't software sold this way? I realize that these tough economic times are generating some large discounts on enterprise software, but the industry by and large charges what it charges. As you know, the profit margins on the sale of software are enormous. Is everyone OK with 60% margins for companies with "soft" in their names? (If you said yes then you're probably OK with the AIG bonuses and our—the American taxpayer—giving money to banks that then lend the money back to us—the American taxpayer—at 14% interest.) I've heard all of the arguments about margins. They're sort of like the arguments the pharmaceutical companies make about their patents and profits. They need all that money to keep the pipeline going. The same argument is used by software vendors: they need high margins so they can reinvest in new and improved software. I'd buy the argument (and maybe even the software) if I saw a continuous release of solid software year after year. But what I see instead is the release of half-baked software that requires service pack after service pack. I also see the entrepreneurial community creating more innovative software than the mainstay vendors in the space. So much for the judicious use of profits.

There are two aspects of this dirty little secret worth noting. The first is the value proposition and the second are the alternatives that still go unexploited by most companies. The historical value proposition of enterprise software is still, to my amazement, alive. Big software vendors produce feature-rich software for huge fees and profits that nearly all of their customers barely use. But the enterprise license is for everyone, even if they never turn on their computers. The pricing models are based upon bundled modules that clients buy if they need them or not. But the not so little secret is that no one has to buy or maintain software anymore. The software-as-a-service delivery model challenges the enterprise licensing model by eliminating it. Add open-source software to the equation and things get very interesting very fast. But not nearly enough of us are working to destroy the old model. Apparently we're still OK with paying through the nose versus paying by the drink. We're also apparently OK with paying for features we never use. When was the last time you used all of the fonts in MS Word or the templates in Excel or the layouts in Powerpoint? You get the idea.

These dirty little secrets represent but a few of the ones that quietly influence decisions and strategies in technology world. Some others to ponder? How about these:

- Many certified project managers have never successfully managed a large project, or anything, for that matter.
- Performance assessments are meaningless when everyone gets the same raise.
- Project scope creep is handled with personnel heroics.
- Very few technology professionals back up their personal files.
- Making the high potential list is a political process.

Maybe we'll examine these some other time.

The takeaways here are clear: do not assume intelligence, competence, or goodwill. Test your colleagues. Are they smart? Or not? Do they know what they're doing? Or not? Are they "good"? Or "evil"? Don't assume that your vendors like or respect you. Identify their vested interests in each of the alternative technology delivery models before breaking bread with them. More to the point, adjust your expectations about your colleagues. Invest in inoffensive, almost polite education. Manipulate the environment. Invest in specific skills such as vendor management and architecture.

CAN YOU HANDLE THE TRUTH?

There's a great scene in the movie, *A Few Good Men,* when Jack Nicholson tells Tom Cruise that he "can't handle the truth." What about you? Can you handle the truth? How honest are you about your ability to deal with the problems that have held business technology optimization back for decades? About people problems that we all know exist but seldom feel comfortable enough to talk about?

I was having dinner with an industry colleague and after a couple of glasses of wine, we started to tell each other the truth (or at least versions of the truth that were much more accurate than the ones exchanged before the wine). I described the conversation to a friend who told me that

I should have recorded it and published it anonymously for everyone to read. Well, here it is.

My colleague described the senior management team at his company as really pretty clueless about computing and communications technology, not in the bits and bytes sense (which, we both agreed, they shouldn't have to understand), but in terms of the strategic relationship between business and technology. Here are some of the observations: "They think technology's a commodity that can be bought at sales." "They think that as machines get more powerful they should cost less and less, and replace more and more people." "They think that consultants know more about the company than we do." "They think that the people who do technology are really not all that good, that all that 'stuff' is way too complicated, way too quirky, unreliable, and way too expensive."

Then he trashed his vendors who seemed to know a lot about processes that he couldn't find at his company, no matter how hard he looked. They also kept him on the upgrade treadmill that was deliberately designed to keep his company in a constant state of churn. Because he lived in a decentralized world, he argued that the ("God-damned") matrix at his company was worse than the one Keanu Reeves surfs around in, that there were just too many people with bold lines and dotted lines running through them, and that no one can have two or three bosses and survive the corporate jungle for very long. Sipping some wine, he matter-of-factly offered, "It's why people who live in matrix organizations eventually go crazy."

As he reached for his fourth glass of wine, he ranted about all of the "killer apps" he has to kill. Seems that there are all kinds of people at the company susceptible to *vendormarketitis*. In the past year alone, he had to kill grid computing, biometric authentication, and even a Segway, among a bunch of other things that the inmates barely understood, but had been told at a cocktail party were killer apps capable of catapulting the company to the "next level."

He railed about his inability to adequately reward excellent, or punish poor, performance, how he had to keep hiring more and more people to do fewer and fewer jobs because he couldn't remove anyone. He said that HR wasn't very helpful here. He wondered aloud what HR actually did at the company.

Charged with developing the company's technology strategy, he asked the people who run strategic planning to define the "as is" and "to be" business models so he could determine which technology investments should and should not be made. But the planners complained that it's impossible to know how the company expects to make money in a few years, that no one can predict the future. When he asked the planners how he was expected to optimize technology investments with less-than-specific information, they persuaded him just to do the best he could, but to make sure that the overall cost of technology went down over time.

Although everyone wanted to "standardize" technologies and processes, no one wanted to play bad cop; in fact, no one even wanted to play good cop. Lip service was all he got. When push came to shove, everyone wanted to call his or her own shots. Every time he tried to enlist the support of senior management to redefine technology governance they ran for the hills. A few months later the same execs asked him to quantify the cost savings attributable to the standardization he had promised.

At this point, I drank a fourth glass of wine. "People," I said, "it's all about the people."

"How long did it take you to figure that out, you idiot," he said. Then he got more serious, turning his guns on the technologists: "The propeller-heads need to understand that technology is only important if it helps business make money. The further removed from that goal they stay, the more irrelevant they are to operations and strategy. Their only job is to make the business successful."

I later shared all this with a vendor friend of mine. "I love how 'vendors' are always the fall-guy. We do the dirty work for lots of companies. We train their people and when money is tight, renegotiate our fees. Where's the problem here? We know the business; it's our job to know the business. Here's a truth: without us, there would be no applications, databases, or net-works. Give me a break. And if he can't tell the difference between a fad and a solution then he's in the wrong business. Killer apps? What is this, 1999?"

So what do we have here: very different cultures, very different agendas, and multiple versions of the truth. And a lot of very odd people.

"Alignment" is like a religious war. But let's talk perspective:

1. The business technology relationship is morphing into a place where everything that isn't overtly strategic is commoditizing. The business performance management trend is about business technology opti-mization or, put another way, alignment on steroids. If you're stuck in the trenches, then you think the senior management team (SMT) is stupid about technology; if you're part of the SMT then you think the people in the trenches just don't get it. The perceptions need to marry, probably with a shotgun.

2. Killer apps are investments that simultaneously reduce costs and increase growth and profitability. If you even think about them without these two goals in mind, then you're hopelessly stuck in the twentieth century, and if you don't think systematically about costs and benefits then you probably shouldn't be in business.

3. People will always be nearly impossible to organize and manage: it makes more sense to accept this rather than to try to change it. The exception to this advice is situational: if your company is tanking then there'll be a bigger appetite to deal honestly and directly with people issues. Seize these moments to do the right thing for the company (and all of the employees expected to work hard to turn things around).

4. If we don't partner well with vendors, we'll ultimately fail. Expertise is specialized and even die-hard in-sourcers will eventually need help. The pace of technology change and the economic pressures over which we have little control will make at least cosourcing inevitable. The key is to partner with vendors who know your sector and technology well. But don't delay. It's essential that you develop a short list of bona fide partners ASAP. But the moment they fail to behave like true partners, shoot them.

5. "Strategy" is owned by everyone. Gone are the days when technology pros can claim that business pros need to prime their agenda with detailed scenarios comprised of business models and processes; business and technology cannot exist without each other. Strategy is a team sport, at least in semi-sane organizations.

I don't think these five "perspectives" are very controversial. Maybe we argue so much because we're under so much stress, or because we've been trained to be suspicious about everyone's motives. All of this stuff is "messy." There's no perfect business model, architecture standardization, or killer app. It's fun to talk about "disruptive" technologies; conversations about balance and compromise are more realistic, more adult. Alignment and optimization are much more about cooperation and negotiation than anything else, and maybe that's all the truth we need. Of course, all of this assumes that the people in your world are capable of cooperation and negotiation. You be the judge. I don't live in your world.

The takeaway? Identify the people in your trenches who can handle the truth and work with them to repackage facts, business cases, and ROI in forms acceptable to those who prefer to ignore the elephants in the room.

The right perspective on vendors, strategy, and even killer apps is essential to transformation of any kind. Everyone complains about just about everything, but it's not all bad. Some of these complaints are therapeutic and some are insightful. Others represent paths to change. Some of your colleagues are beyond hope (and investment) but others are salvageable. Identify the permanent losers and invest in the possible. Develop some tests to separate the hopeless from the hopeful. For example, present some new directions and gauge how accepting each of your colleagues is to the proposals. Those who insist on throwing you-know-what on the ideas are the losers. Those who embrace the ideas as possible, even exciting, are the keepers. You get the idea. The tough part is to separate those who accept the truth from those who don't and then treat the two classes of people very differently. Can you do that?

WHEN REASON, LOGIC, AND BUSINESS CASES FAIL

Stupid executives, paranoid CEOs, greedy managers: they're everywhere. How many personal agendas can we take?

Look, we all know what I'm talking about. It would be acceptable if this were just about mediocrity versus excellence, but it's about much more than that. It's about evil, self-serving mediocrity (or outright evil, self-serving incompetence). It's about what the military tries to avoid at all cost: stupid arrogant officers. Implicitly this means that it's OK to be stupid and OK to be arrogant, but that the combination of the two is deadly and, in the military, can actually get people killed. In the technology trenches people don't get killed (although sometimes they lose their jobs), but they do get marginalized, discarded, and disrespected, often for all the wrong reasons. When this happens what should you do?

Some suggest it's best just to keep your mouth shut, bide your time, and hope that the idiot gets promoted, fired, or hit by a truck. But others suggest that you attack the bastards. How might that work? Your first weapon is evidence. If the boss says that you should outsource technology to Mumbai or the Philippines without a business case, then you should build that business case and present it to the boss as often as you can. Of course she may dismiss it, but the effort will establish you as an evidence-based annoyance and, because of the dismissal, release you to undermine your boss. This can be accomplished in several ways. You can anonymously release the business case to your boss' boss. You can build support for the case with your colleagues. You can use the vendors that stand to lose if the outsourcing occurs to bang on your boss and your boss' bosses. You can turn the issue into a tough political campaign.

Am I kidding? Not at all. You have only two choices when stupid technology decisions are made. You can (1) ignore the decisions or (2) you can push back. Candidly, most all of us ignore the stupid decisions in favor of covering our own asses, protecting our jobs, and avoiding confrontation. But the pushback does not have to be confrontational; it can be clandestine and manipulative. Look at the roles that "surrogates" play in the current presidential election campaign.

I have seen some unbelievable things in my career, things I wish I had attacked, in every way possible, at the time. Some years ago I watched a CIO/CFO relationship turn on fishing trips: decisions that made no sense were wrapped in new fishing rods and reels. The approach worked because the CFO had a limited knowledge of technology and loved fishing in exotic places. (Like you, I have seen similar strategies work with wine, golf, and football.) I listened incredulously when a global CIO of an enormous company told me that if all I could save him was $250,000,000 a year (yes, the number is correct) he wasn't interested because of the political fights that the path to savings would trigger. I've watched start-up CEOs buy enterprise database and ERP licenses from Oracle, IBM, and SAP (for their 10 employees) and I've seen venture capitalist after venture capitalist ruin solid technology companies with their "wisdom" about what the technology offerings of the companies should look like.

I give myself a solid "C" for my reactions to these kinds of events. I left one of the above companies, refused to consult to another, and worked the halls for anyone who would listen with yet another. But I always drew a line in the sand that was, ultimately, self-serving. I left the first company for a better company, walked away from the consulting gig that would have been incredibly frustrating and borderline fraudulent, and stopped well short of mining or barbed-wiring the halls, instead doing my "dirty work" over fancy comfortable (company-paid) breakfasts, lunches, and dinners.

So what am I suggesting? Guerilla warfare. I am recommending that we attack stupid, greedy, deranged executives with every weapon we can find. Frontal attacks as well as rear action strategies are equally effective. If the culture is openly punitive, then frontal attacks may be too dangerous. So attack from the rear: undermine the stupidity, discredit the source, and end-run the decision makers. Elevate the debate (does the board of directors know what's going on?). Do what it takes to shine a very bright light on stupidity, arrogance, and personal greed.

Some of you will see this as treason: demeaning and cynical. But the fact is that really stupid decisions can actually threaten the survival of a company. Hundreds of millions and even billions of dollars are often at stake. Should we keep our mouths shut? Or should we fight fire with fire? Is it about the individuals—you, me, and the idiots—or the company and the jobs, products, and services it provides? You decide. And when all else fails, invoke all of the evil soft skills you can muster. See below for some instructions.

SOFT SKILLS FROM THE DARK SIDE

I have another friend (who also likes wine) who has three rules of business: "People suck, people suck, and people suck." Sure, he's a little paranoid, but he's also essentially correct (reminding us that even paranoid people can have real enemies). Most of the problems we face as professional business technologists are related to people and their personalities, biases, and intellectual abilities, among other features unique to the human species. There are so many jerks out there that it's impossible to know how to survive, especially if your company is jerk-prone. And there are lots of jerk-prone companies.

There are a couple of ways to go here. The first tried and true way is to complain incessantly about the idiots, jerks, and narcissists. We're well aware of this approach. Many of your colleagues have perfected this approach after years (and in some cases decades) of honing just the right complaint twang. Complaining all the time can actually make you feel good, depending upon your own personality, but it can also make you depressed inasmuch as the complaining doesn't actually change anything. It also attracts the wrong kind of attention: even when complaints are justified, no one likes to hear them.

The other way to go is to identify and implement a set of manipulative soft skills designed to get you what you want. Manipulative? Absolutely. Soft skills? We all know what they are, but many of us just can't master them. Why not? Because we don't have the personalities? Because they're too difficult to learn? No, because we're just not motivated.

So let's get this out of the way right now. Many of us are unwilling to kiss ass, work the troops, sandbag, or play politics not because we can't, but because we don't want to. You have to decide what you want to accomplish and the tools you'd like to use to achieve the results you deem important. We've already dismissed the complaining tool. Now we can examine some other tools, the soft skills from the dark side.

We all know the kissing ass tool. If we're honest, we'll admit to using the tool in our personal relationships: it's a rare friend or spouse who hasn't kissed ass at some point to get what he or she wants. But in the workplace, it's more complicated. It's a tool that can make insecure managers and executives feel good about themselves and therefore about the ass kisser. But on the other hand, use of this tool means that you have to swallow truth and objectivity and fawn all over stupid, nasty idiots and jerks who clearly don't deserve any form of respect or adulation. Can you do this? There's a credibility issue at work here. If you compliment idiots for doing stupid things, does that make you an idiot?

Regardless, ass kissing can be very effective, especially if done in private. Credibility (and other things) suffers when you kiss ass in public. Don't do it. I knew a guy who kissed so much public ass that we used to handicap when his head would bury itself, well, you know where. Consequently, no one took the guy seriously (except himself and the asses he kissed; BTW, he's done very well for himself; in fact, he's a multimillionaire.)

This political tool is hard to use. Sort of like a 64-degree wedge (if you play golf). But once mastered it can be extremely effective. The first step here is to profile the players. Who's got power? Who are the boss' friends? Who will be the next VP? Who's on his way out? It's essential that you get this right. Once you're confident about the players and their positions, map out their individual strategies. Then locate all of the intersections on the maps. The game is played from the intersecting points on the maps of the current and projected power brokers. Make sure that you cater to them and their objectives. You can ignore (insult, if you're bold) those falling from grace. Always use the profiles, maps, and intersecting points to make even the simplest moves.

Good consultants know how to underpromise and overdeliver. It's a good practice. The trick is to sandbag just enough to stay out of trouble. Make sure that you always deliver but don't underpromise so much that it looks as if you're overprotecting your flanks. Image management is the objective: you want the power players to think you deliver, get it done, and can be trusted to consistently come through, without being a threat to the insecure SMT.

The skill here is to make everyone think you're leading when in fact you're leading at cross-purposes. Your project team thinks you're in their corner leading them to victory, but the managers understand that your team is far from perfect and if it wasn't for you they might very well fail. You get the idea.

So that's the short list of soft skills from the dark side or, if you prefer, evil soft skills. But just so you don't think I only value evil soft skills, there are good soft skills such as project/program management, negotiations, communications, and, of course, good hard skills such as specific technology skills, that are almost as important as the evil ones. But when push comes to shove in corporate America, it's often better to be evil than good. Sorry, idealists. But I'm still trying to figure out why people who wreck companies get $100,000,000 rewards. Or why CEOs who erode market share and market capitalization are treated as heroes by their boards of directors and the compensation committees that gild every aspect of their existence. Yeah, I'm really angry about these and lots of other things. Aren't you? (You're not? Then you really need to keep reading this book.)

WHAT WILL YOU (REALLY) BE DOING IN A FEW YEARS?

OK, so you're feeling a little better these days since technology spending has stabilized somewhat (which means that the decreases are smaller than they've been). Your company seems to have a handle on what the "new" IT strategy should look like (mostly infrastructure projects, very few big strategic initiatives, and very little training around emerging technologies [inasmuch as they're unlikely to be deployed]). But don't believe the calm. IT's really just before the storm.

So what do you think? What will you be doing in a few years? Will you be doing network management, PC deployment, break and fix, server maintenance, applications development, sitting behind a help desk, plodding through data in search of business intelligence (BI), or what? And where will you be doing whatever it is you end up doing?

The trends are very clear, so listen up. Although there will always be a tremendous need to "run the engine" (keep operational technology going), where that takes place is changing dramatically. Providers are leaving the vertical corporate nests for outsourcer opportunities. This is not all bad for internal IT professionals who work in infrastructure. Their jobs will not go away; they will just move. Sometimes they will move down the street but sometimes they will move across the planet.

So if you're in the infrastructure business you should track trends here and prepare to look good to outsourcers who will need your skills to deliver operational technology to their clients. Do not expect to end your careers—unless you're a couple of years from retirement (!)—at your pharmaceutical, financial services, retail, chemical, or manufacturing company. Your infrastructure services are horizontal, not vertical, and therefore commodities, and commodities usually travel a lot.

Who's left inside and what will they be doing? Inside technologists will become more strategic and performance focused. Some will work in architecture, some in social media, some in vendor management, some in requirements and demand management, and some in budgeting. The architects will don white coats and walk around pontificating about SOA, EDA, open-source APIs, and business processes. They will be highly paid and interface extensively with the vendor community about technology trends. They will manage enterprise architecture as well as how that dovetails with the functional (communications, applications, data) architectures. This is heady stuff and requires a lot of ongoing learning and thinking. Architects are probably the most cerebral professionals in our world, although that should not discourage you from morphing into a brainy architect (after all, George Constanza pretended to be an architect for years).

The social mediaphiles will explore all things Web 2.0, 3.0, 4.0, and eventually 5.0. More and more transactions are moving to the web. Gen X and (especially) Y live on the web. Customer service, innovation, content management, training, and a whole range of additional activities will move to the web. The optimization of collaboration and content that social media enables will become a corporate priority. How many of us really understand social media and its implications for business? Social media knowledge and skills are already in very short supply.

Vendor managers can write their own tickets, real vendor managers, that is. There are certifications in vendor management, negotiations, SLA management, performance management, ITIL, CoBIT, and related areas that "qualify" professionals as legitimate vendor managers. If you invest in this knowledge and these skills you will be rewarded. Because there are hardly any good vendor managers out there, this skill set is a green field of opportunity. Seize it, assuming that you like it.

Requirements and demand management represent a skill set that essentially manages the technology demand and fulfillment process. But in order to do this well professionals need to understand several domains. First, they need to understand business processes and models, deeply.

Second, it requires knowledge of existing technology and the potential of that technology to satisfy requirements. Next they need to understand the allocation of talent to tasks and how to optimize the project and program management processes. Yes, that's a lot of knowledge and even more skills. How many of us have this knowledge or these skills?

Finally, IT finance will become more and more important as we segment operational and strategic technology, outsource more and more, and manage our vendors to cost–performance metrics. Specialists in this area will become increasingly valuable to companies that need to optimize their technology investments.

These are the areas that will pay the big bucks in the next few years and probably through 2020. After that, who the hell knows. But if you want to gear up for the next decade, these five areas will serve you well.

THE (REALLY) PERFECT CIO (YOU KNOW THE TYPE)

If I read another article about "the new CIO" or "CIOs in transition," or "CIO challenges" I will volunteer to be waterboarded and tell everyone what I really think about stating the obvious. Here's the drivel that comes out of the industry's "press":

- CIOs should understand the business.
- CIOs should understand technology.
- CIOs should practice management best practices.
- CIOs should have good communications skills.
- CIOs should be good leaders.

Lists like these remind me of the television commercial that has the golfer Phil Michelson sitting with his fans who have agreed to offer him some advice: "I think you should hit the ball farther," the first fan says. Then the other fan says, "I think you should hit it straighter." "Longer and straighter." Phil says, "Really helpful … got it."

Chief information officers, especially when they are part of their company's executive council (EC), should (although many don't; see below for why they get to commit ignorance with impunity) know all of the above and then some. Do we really need to tell them what they should already know? Do I have to read articles, year after year, that list the skills and competencies that CIOs should have to be "successful"? It's almost as though their editors have given every cub reporter the same rite-of-passage assignment: "Go forth and tell the world what the CIO should be able to do and we will publish your take (the 1,000,000th take) on what the perfect CIO should look like."

So let's describe the *really* perfect CIO. I will not be providing another obvious list of skills and competencies. Instead, I'll profile the nuances that make all the difference in the world. I am assuming that they already know (something at least) about business, technology, and management. I realize that this assumption is flawed; however, I just cannot state the obvious again. So let's go with the counterintuitive and the unspoken dirty-little-secret-based reality of executive qualities in twenty-first-century America. In fact, really perfect CIOs can whiff all of the above competencies if they master the following.

First and foremost, regardless of the sex of the CIO, there must be really good hair. Bald CIOs, CIOs with hard hair, and CIOs whose hair has multiple colors cannot succeed. Although good hair is not necessary and sufficient for success (note Mitt Romney's failed presidential bid even with the world's best hair), it's a strong predictor of success. (Don't believe me? How many bald presidents have we had? Reagan had great hair. Kennedy's was even better. Bill Clinton's hair was good. Carter's was OK. The Bush boys also had good hair. Obama's hair is the perfect length and color. Only Gerald Ford and Dwight Eisenhower were bald, but Ford was never elected president and Eisenhower was a war hero [who is allowed to be bald]).

Next comes the smile. It needs to appear to be genuine, exposing very white teeth. If you're a CIO and you haven't had your teeth whitened, it's time to visit the dentist. Smiling faces make people happy. Frowning faces, even if there's good reason to frown, make people uneasy. "He's miserable!" These are two words you do not want people to mutter when you enter a room.

Clothes are hugely important. They have to be just expensive enough to avoid envy and anger. These days, clothes should be understated but tasteful. But what's "tasteful"? Check out what the boss wears and crank it back one notch, a little less expensive and a little less "look-at-me." Don't vote for casual Fridays (or any casual days). They're for the masses, not the bosses.

Golf is a prerequisite. If you don't hold a 15 or under handicap then you need to get some lessons, practice hard, and join the right country club.

Once you get the number down to 10 you can command a significant audience on the course consisting of important members of the EC. But the really perfect CIO knows enough to miss the five-foot putt on the last hole to lose the match to the slightly better dressed CEO.

The ability to tell colorful and off-color jokes is also extremely important. A repertoire of exciting stories makes all the difference when the conversation turns boring. Really perfect CIOs keep some jokes on the palms of their hands, just in case.

Really perfect CIOs must actually have personalities. They must be people who consume more than oxygen in a room. The really perfect CIO commands attention, respect, and, through a modicum of charisma, generates as much heat as light. Fun people who can hold their own in a conversation, bars, and even on the dance floor are more likely to succeed than CIOs who mumble, don't drink, and can't dance.

It goes without saying that really perfect CIOs are glib as hell. They also do not speak truth-to-power, are never abrasive, and make certain that their personal hygiene is impeccable. They are dispassionate leaders who know when to keep their mouths shut (which, they've figured out, is most of the time). Really perfect CIOs have broken the success code: do what you're told by people who can promote and reward you. Never threaten them with politics, intelligence, or thinly veiled references to Julie in accounting.

You get the picture. Really perfect CIOs know a few things about business and technology but the really successful CIOs dress, talk, smile, joke, golf, and smell really good, and let's not forget the hair.

WILL YOU WORK FOR RESULTS?

Everyone says they prefer meritocracies to the political messes they find themselves cleaning up every day. Really? How about performance-based compensation? Could you live with that?

Not long ago I pitched a consulting project to a very large company that I knew had some huge problems with how they did technology. I identified a number of areas where they needed help and where they could save a lot of money (I mean a lot of money: in the hundreds of millions of dollars) annually. When I told them my fee to save them money, they decided to skip the project. So I asked them if they would fund the project as a percentage of what I actually saved them, not on any kind of fee basis. After I explained several times that they only had to pay me if I saved them money, they rejected the project again. Can you think of anything wrong with paying me, or anyone, based on their actual performance? I guess we're just too used to pitchers, wide receivers, and point guards making tons of money even if they fail to perform. What a gig! They get to under-perform and underachieve, year after year, and still make millions and millions of dollars. Apparently, we're all OK with this, because we keep paying ever-increasing ticket prices to see underachieving professional athletes with other obvious problems deliver lackluster performances. Similarly, it appears we're OK with paying executives millions and mil-lions of dollars to ruin public companies. Why not pay athletes and CEOs for performance? A-Rod should get a base pay with a huge kicker for per-formance. But if he fails to hit any home runs then he would make rela-tively little money. Let's negotiate with him on the bonus around homers, not for just showing up (or hanging out with Madonna).

How about paying CIOs for performance? Why not set some metrics for making and saving money with technology and pay them accord-ingly? The trades just published the list of the most highly paid CIOs and I noticed that many of them worked for companies that haven't done so well recently (or since the CIOs have been there). These CIOs probably wouldn't like performance-based pay; or would they? What if you were compensated at 5% of what you saved a company in annual technology expenditures? Let's assume that the company spends a billion dollars a year on technology. Would you take the deal? Or, like a lot of lawyers, doc-tors, CEOs, senators, and congressmen, would you prefer to get paid lots of money regardless of how well you perform? Sort of like it is today?

Shared-risk contracting is another flavor of performance-based com-pensation. If you hire an outsourcer to support your infrastructure but they screw it up should you pay them? What if they refuse to work under any kind of shared-risk arrangement? Should you hire them to do any-thing at all? Seems to me that outsourcers who fail to hit the metrics in your service-level agreements should pay dearly, not just in threats to not renew their contracts but where it hurts. How about if a 5% "miss" that results in no fees until the problems are corrected (with, of course, abso-lutely no profit accruing to the outsourcer for the incompetence). Let's put 33% of every month's fees in escrow and release the money only when the SLAs have been audited. I like that approach. It's always better to hold the money when there might be a problem than dispersing it and then trying to get it back.

Hardware and software vendors should also be paid according to their performance. If the software they sell us fails to solve our problems should we still have to pay them? If PCs, servers, and other devices fail to deliver then why should we pay for them? What about all of the amazing promises CRM, ERP, and other vendors make about their products? Why can't we hold them accountable for what their code actually does for, and to, us?

True story: a couple of years ago I sent half of my cell phone bill to my carrier with a note that explained inasmuch as the phone only worked half the time I should only have to pay half the bill. Of course they ignored my note and carried over the unpaid bill to the next month. So I tried it again but this time I got a call that explained that if I wanted to keep my cell phone I'd better pay the bill. I was told that I was free to call each time a call was dropped, although I'd be charged for the minutes I used to complain. Phone companies don't like performance-based fees. Cable companies don't like it either. How many of us really do?

What about taking performance-based pay into the trenches? What about paying people for what they produce? Programmers, network managers, database administrators, web designers, and customer service representatives could all make a lot of money exceeding performance metrics for their specific areas of expertise, or not, if they hang up on their customers.

Another true story: I was caught in the Air France strike last year and could not get out of the country. No one called me to tell me that my flight had been cancelled, not Air France or American Express which had booked the business trip for me. When I called for help to get home I was told I'd have to wait a week or more as I was staring at a screen from Orbitz telling me that if I really wanted to I could leave Paris in three hours. I told the AMEX travel "consultant" this and she told me that Orbitz could not book my flight home. When I suggested she go to the site, she hung up on me! (So I just booked the trip through Orbitz and got home with no problems.) Should Air France and AMEX get paid well for this performance? Where is the accountability? Technology lends itself to incentive-based pay because the results of our work can be quantified. But how many of us would live this way?

Here's how it should work:

1. The metrics you would like to use to determine how much money you make (or don't make) depending on your performance should be defined. Be generous here. If you think that you should be paid $25 an hour for mediocre work but $200 for truly excellent work, then you should define the mediocre/excellent continuum with specific performance metrics. If you are a high-level, well-paid technology manager then your numbers will be much higher.
2. Vendors should step up to shared-risk contracting and pure performance-based compensation. (This may be my last book after the vendor community organizes my demise.)
3. Technology executives, especially CIOs and CTOs, should be compensated based on how much money they save (without compromising service) and how much money they make with technology.

Do you like this or do you hate this? For it to work it has to be universal: everyone in the organization has to be paid according to her actual performance. Put another way, we should strive to invalidate Woody Allen's famous quote: "80% of success in life is just showing up." Want to suggest this to your schizophrenic boss?

The principle is the important aspect of all this. Do you think that there's an appetite for working and being rewarded for results? The discussion at least should occur to test the performance-based compensation waters. If the culture goes into cardiac arrest just from the discussion, then it's a good bet that it's not ready for actually paying people for what they do (versus for the space they occupy).

SOMETIMES YOU MUST GO NEGATIVE

I've had it with our inability to get things done; our inability to acknowledge the real reasons why our field's best practices get crippled the moment a meeting begins. Do we actually know what to do? Do we know how to optimize our IT investments? Of course we do. So what keeps us from getting the most out of IT?

Let's start with management, not IT management—we'll get to that next—but to corporate management. By and large, nontechnology managers, directors, and executives do not understand IT beyond its ability to support e-mail, spreadsheets, and occasionally financial dashboards.

Many of them think that IT is easy, too slow, costs too much, and is too unreliable. Although I'd be the last one to suggest that nontechnology managers go back to school, it is their responsibility to invest in understanding the basics around operational and especially strategic technology. Management should not spend time educating themselves; they should be open to learning more about the intersection of their business models and current and emerging technologies. If I hear another nontechnology executive tell me that he "had no idea" how technology is delivered at his company or the alternative delivery models that can really juice the business, I will scream and shove a server right up his business. One only gets to plead ignorance for so long.

Then there are the IT professionals who refuse to accept their roles as support, as enablers of tactical and strategic business transactions. Instead, they want the same respect as the salesperson who lands a lucrative $10,000,000 contract with a client, a multiyear manufacturing partnership, or finds just the right company to acquire. The truth is that there's business and there's technology and until technology directly drives revenue it will play a supporting role. IT professionals: get over it, or build a killer cross-selling or up-selling platform that drives significant profitable growth. Otherwise, keep quiet and deliver world-class infrastructure and applications services. Trust me, if you want a seat at the big table you have to gild it in gold you personally mine. But if you do discover gold along the way, you will quickly become the most popular guy at whatever table you want.

How about our inability to pursue the right projects or kill bad ones? Why is that so hard? How many certified project managers does it take to kill a bad project? So a business case goes bad. So what? Kill the project. Part of the reason why IT often has a bad reputation is because it fails to deliver projects on time and within budget, and it often fails to deliver because bad projects stay in the pipeline. We need to learn how to kill bad projects or to accept the effect bad projects have on our professional credibility. I am sick and tired of people who want it both ways.

Then there are the embedded contradictions and inconsistencies in our processes that we pretend don't exist. What am I talking about here? How about discretionary versus nondiscretionary budgets? There are no discretionary budgets. Everything is eaten by nondiscretionary hardware, software, and services. Project management? What project management? How many of your certified PMOs are certifiably insane? Project management looks great on paper but try finding professionals who know how to identify, sell, manage, fix, and kill projects? What about standardization versus agility? Everyone knows that the business unit with the biggest profits makes the rules, even if it means yielding to "standards" and other annoying rules.

Vendors also make me angry. Not the small ones trying hard to get our business or blaze a new technology trail, but the big entrenched ones that see us as dependent on their products and services. Especially egregious are the large enterprise software vendors that still (can you imagine?) in the on-demand era expect us to pay huge annual maintenance fees and then upgrade fees or they charge us extra just to keep the old stuff running, until we have no financial choice but to upgrade and begin the maintenance cost cycle all over again. Once the software-as-a-service (SaaS) model is perfected, there will be hell to pay: the corporate CIOs I work with will jump ship so fast their vendors' heads will spin. Time to short enterprise software stocks? Oracle, SAP, and Microsoft really need to rethink their fee structures. On-demand applications, open-source software, and the growing repository of web-based components will threaten existing software delivery models to the breaking point. Do the vendors really understand this, or are they in denial? They say the right things, but they're still addicted to enterprise license fees. Don't let them get away with it.

Lastly, let's acknowledge that most of our leadership is pretty self-absorbed. I tell my students that the best path to corporate influence is through personal bonuses and compensation packages. This is equivalent to modeling managers and executives as self-serving, self-interested actors who respond well to financial incentives but don't react that well to initiatives that only help the company. Like public company CFOs, they focus squarely on short-term gratification and initiatives that put money into their pockets. What else do you need to know about business technology "alignment"? Please.

What did I miss? Rants are therapeutic. I feel better already. You need to rant from time to time as well. The key is to make the rants purposeful.

PAY VERY CLOSE ATTENTION TO NEW ERA SKILLS

We're in another "new era." Technology is changing so rapidly that managers in the trenches have to respond to yet another "sea change." When will it end? (Never, but you already knew that.) Take a look at Figure 1.1,

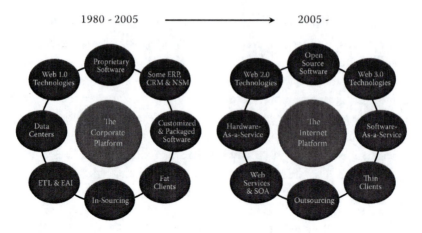

FIGURE 1.1
Trends and skills.

which communicates the changes that have occurred just over the past few years, changes that require lots of new skills.

Figure 1.1 suggests that the Internet will become the dominant platform of the early twenty-first century. If the trends in the figure are accurate, whole new knowledge and skill sets will be necessary to exploit the trends that ultimately will help the business achieve its goals.

So what are these skills? Here are some that will drive the changes implied by Figure 1.1:

1. Due diligence, or the ability to objectively assess alternative technologies, technology delivery models, and business technology performance
2. Enterprise architecture, or the ability to understand where business processes and technology functionality actually meet
3. Technology service models such as software/hardware as services, communications service models, and support service models
4. Vendor management, or the ability to develop RFPs, SLAs, and ROI, especially for infrastructure, architecture, and security outsourcing
5. Interoperability and integration, or the ability to exploit standards such as web services, service-oriented architectures, and event-driven architecture
6. Abstractions-into-solutions, or the ability to understand concept shifts such as virtualization, the Internet as an operating system, and data as prescriptions for profitable growth

7. Artificial intelligence (AI), or the engine that will drive Web 3.0
8. Project and program management, or the ability to understand and measure execution regardless of whether it's done by in-house professionals or outside partners
9. Access device strategy, or the ability to optimize the use of other-than-PC devices to get to networks, data, and applications
10. Business intelligence, or the ability to understand the contribution that analytics of all kinds can make to business performance

These are just a few of the skills you'll need to succeed. Going forward we need to make sure that we develop these skills in our professionals and that we evaluate "technologists" according to how well these skills are represented in our companies. What else should go on the list? What's the point? If Figure 1.1 isn't a wake-up call I have no idea how to resuscitate you. Stay sleeping or evolve yourself and your team. It's not as if you have a choice. Send HR a copy of Figure 1.1. See if HR gets IT. Figure 1.1 is the skills roadmap for you, your team, and your company. Conduct a skills inventory as soon as possible, and continuously, and then develop a learning strategy to close the skills gaps the inventory reveals. The inventory should be conducted by an independent third party and the results should not be reported quietly on a small paper napkin. Everyone should know about the skills, the gaps, and the plans to fill them. Education, training, rotation, mentoring, and any other step that makes sense should be considered.

You cannot run from this job, so take it seriously. Without the right people doing the right things with the right skills, you will fail.

Everyone to the Woodshed

I'm angry about our inability to police ourselves against self-inflicted wounds. I've been at this for a lot of years and I cannot believe how often the same problems repeat themselves and how otherwise impressive companies find it impossible to get the most basic things right. Why is the business technology learning curve so damn flat?

Not long ago I visited a large company that had 11 ERPs systems and 19 instances of them. Shortly after that I found myself talking with technology executives about their failed attempts to standardize their hardware, and right after that I helped a company think about how they should train their business technology professionals to think more about the business value of technology. I then found myself talking with some CIOs about whether they should think about outsourcing desktop support and their help desks. Is it me, or are these issues something like 20 years old? Where the hell has everyone been, and why is it still so hard to practice discipline in the acquisition, deployment, and support of technology?

I told the CIO of the company with the 11/19 ERP problem that I could guarantee $250,000,000 to the company's bottom line if he'd agree to practice some discipline (yes, the same $250,000,000 I discussed previously). I know, I know, you think that $250,000,000 is an exaggeration: I assure you it's not. The company in question has an annual global IT budget of over $2,000,000,000 and is wasting a ton of money on the installation, support, and maintenance of unnecessary hardware and software. I could guarantee a $250,000,000 savings if the company committed to a disciplined approach to standardization and deployment that would forbid the deployment of redundant applications. Hell, I even offered to forgo a consulting fee to make it happen, offering instead to take a percentage of the savings that were actually achieved: a completely risk-free deal. They declined. Why?

Why do companies continue to make the same mistakes year after year? Well, the answer is almost too simple and equally exasperating: they just can't bring themselves to tell people things they don't want to hear. Reducing the number of ERP applications might upset some people, I was told. Standardization makes people angry. "People don't like being told what to do," I've been told a million times. Of course, these same people complain all the time about the cost of technology, arguing that IT should be cheaper every year because, after all, IT has all been commoditized.

Enough of this stupidity. We all learn early in life that we can't have it both ways. Either we adhere to best practices or we pay the price. I resent management's insistence that technology costs be reduced when they fail to discipline the acquisition, deployment, or support processes. I resent the CIOs and CTOs who don't have the courage to make the tough political calls when their corporate cultures might support these calls. There's no excuse for the lack of discipline that leads to avoiding tough conversations with the boys, who I guess might not tell the bearer of bad news about Saturday's tee time. An even more serious concern is among the shareholders of public companies that waste millions and in some cases billions of dollars on perfectly avoidable technology mistakes. Who's accountable to them?

It's epidemic. Too many companies have too many applications, too many servers, and too many laptops. Too many CIOs are afraid to make anyone mad. Too many CEOs fail to demand discipline from their technology executives, yet still complain about technology costs. Much of the "technology-is-hard" crowd doesn't pay enough attention to the lack of discipline that makes IT so hard.

It's not about performance, reliability or even security. These are solvable problems. The really tough problems are exacerbated by lack of will, poor discipline, our need to be liked, our tendency to avoid conflict, just about everyone's desire to take the easy way out, and our desire to dodge accountability whenever we can. No one thinks he will end up in a woodshed. Maybe we should bring it back.

Accountability is the key. But many corporate cultures, not to mention the people that define them, won't even discuss accountability. Will you? Will your company? What happens when someone walks away from a $250,000,000 annual cost savings? Does she keep her job? Or does she get a larger bonus? What happens when your favorite quarterback throws more interceptions than any other quarterback? Does he make less money? What happens when a CEO wrecks a company, does he still get a bonus and, ultimately, a gorgeous golden parachute? The toughest thing about corporate accountability is the lack of national accountability. When there's no precedent for fairness, it's tough to start a new one. But that said, you should try to introduce the notions of accountability, discipline, and even performance-based compensation into your world. You won't get as far as you may like, but you might just ever-so-slightly change the culture enough to change the way people see the relationships among work, performance, and rewards.

Politics, Culture, and You

I teach an Executive MBA class at Villanova University on business technology optimization. The course looks at emerging business models, technologies, and technology management best practices, and ways to optimize the interrelationships across all of these areas. Something happened recently in one of my classes that I think deserves some discussion.

While wrapping up the semester's work one of the students challenged me and the group: "Sure, all of this stuff is good, and powerful, and might even contribute to the business, but when all's said and done politics determines what gets funded and what gets killed, what the company does and what it doesn't do. Good arguments are nice, but they usually fall on deaf ears. ... I'd rather play golf with the boss than work my ass off writing the 'perfect' business case." When I failed to respond immediately (not that I disagreed with the comments) several others chimed in, agreeing that it was mostly, if not all, "political" out there, and that if you weren't a political player you were doomed.

Are we doomed? Is it all about who you know, not what you know? Does politics explain what happens and what doesn't? The premise of organic management is that people, processes, organizations, and corporate cultures explain more of the impact that technology has than technology itself.

First, it's important to assess the political quotient of your company. Some companies are almost completely "political": a few people make decisions based only on what they think, who they like (and dislike), and based on what's good for them personally (which may or may not be good for the company). This is ground zero. It gets no worse than this. On the other extreme are companies that are obsessive-compulsive about data, evidence, and analysis. Sometimes they're so compulsive they fail to make any decisions at all! In the middle are most of the companies out there, with some balance between analysis and politics. Where is your company on this continuum? It's important to locate your company accurately. It's also important to locate your own preferences, your own culture. The gap between your personal culture and your corporate culture is what will keep you sane or drive you crazy.

The discussion with the students moved quickly toward a discussion of alternative corporate cultures and the personalities that each culture breeds. Technology decisions in analytical cultures tend to be driven by (usually half-baked, but still baked, nonetheless) TCO and ROI calculations, but technology decisions in highly political cultures often have bad outcomes because technology decisions are frequently complicated and expensive. (Remember the $500,000,000?) Industry analysts have told us for years that somewhere around 75% of all big technology projects fail. I suspect that if we correlated this finding with corporate culture we'd find some interesting things.

We also talked about personal preferences. What kind of culture do you like? Some of us flourish in politically charged cultures, whereas others thrive in analytical cultures. The key is the gap between where you live and who you are. (I will refrain from commenting on those who thrive in purely political cultures. You know who you are, and you know how you survive, you ass-kissing glib bastards.)

I ended the class with a discussion about how holistic business technology decisions really are (not with a discussion about how to neutralize political decision making or change corporate cultures). At the heart of the matter is the balance between analysis and politics or, expressed more gently, research and philosophy. For example, business technology decisions occur within a philosophical context often expressed in dicta such as, "We don't believe in off-shore outsourcing," or "We never build applications; we always buy and integrate them."

These kinds of philosophical preferences drive the technology agenda. Decisions that make the list are then approached analytically or politically, depending on the culture. Maneuvering through decision-making mazes can be challenging or rewarding, depending on the size of your personal/corporate culture gap.

Bottom line? If you're political but your culture is analytical, or vice versa, it may be time to move. But if you're aligned with your culture, you should prosper. The matrix looks something like Figure 1.2. Highly political people in totally political cultures eventually lose their minds, but that's just my opinion; I could be wrong. What worries me most are the people and cultures that are part political and part analytical. How do they make decisions without arguing with their companies and themselves? Enough. Where do you want to live? What kind of culture are you? I think you get the picture.

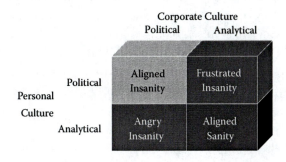

FIGURE 1.2
Where do you live?

Can You Smell Change?

Nicholas Carr, again; outsourcing, identity theft, security, again; wireless, web services, service-oriented architectures, Longhorn, then Vista, then 7 (then 8, 9, and 10); RFID, again. If we were pattern recognition experts, what would we see? "Nothing," you would say, "It's all chaos!"

What the hell is going on in our industry, anyway? Here are three things to think about. Should we be happy or worried?

The Consolidating Technology Industry

CISCO continues to gobble up companies and even service companies are attracting mergers and acquisitions, and everyone's already heard too much about Oracle's slate of acquisitions. Will this trend continue? Yes, with a vengeance. Why? Because commoditization of infrastructure products and services especially is continuing with a vengeance. Differentiation in this space is tough; it's even tougher to generate profits from commodities, which require scale to make money. What does consolidation mean to us? Fewer choices (such as what the cable TV industry gives us) and even fewer bells and whistles. The change is in the distribution of power among the vendors. First, fewer vendors now have more power; second, fewer powerful vendors means less competition and eventually higher prices (or at least less negotiating room). Is this good for the industry? Well, it's good for the deep-pocket survivors but ultimately bad for the consumers of technology products and services. If we fast forward 20 years, technology consumers will be screaming for more government regulation of technology utilities. All of this suggests that you pick your vendors carefully and track the macro trends that define the structure of the technology industry.

Major Changes in the Value and Location of Skill Sets

Undergraduates (and their parents) actually understood this earlier than industry pundits. Voting with their feet, thousands abandoned the technology majors, including computer science, software engineering, and management information systems. They saw the handwriting on the wall years ago, when technology and business process outsourcing began to increase so dramatically. Programming expertise is far less valuable in the United States today than it was in the 1980s or 1990s. Much of it is leaving the United States for cheaper pastures. It will never return. The only refuge is in skill sets such as advanced architecture and complex data integration and mining, areas less likely to be commoditized because they grow from digital technology innovation which is, for the moment at least, still largely led by the United States. The problem is that the education and training industries are not responding quickly enough to reorient students to different careers. If educational and training programs remain in the twentieth century, there will be no valuable skills to market.

Innovation at Risk

Technology companies are hoarding huge stockpiles of cash. Why? Probably because they have less confidence in future revenue than they are revealing. Why not use the cash for more R&D? The Bush administration influenced spending reductions in basic research through the National Science Foundation (NSF) and the Defense Advanced Research Projects Agency (DARPA) in computer science and information technology. The Obama administration is reversing the trend. Years ago DARPA funded the lion's share of PhDs in the field, but no more. The private equity venture capital crowd is investing less and less in seed and early stage companies and thereby depriving them of innovation capital. This has already had a profound effect on computing and communications technology innovation. Instead of risking capital on seed and early stage companies (which, incidentally, have higher historical returns than later stage companies) they are behaving more and more like conservative bankers (who prefer to loan money to people who don't really need it). These trends plus the undergraduate boycott of technology majors will create an innovation drought.

Is there any good news? Yes, operational technology is now cheaper and more reliable than it's ever been. We have management best practices that actually make a lot of sense, things such as standardization, project and portfolio management, vendor management, and the like. Integration and interoperability technology are evolving. Whole new hardware and software architectures, which will stimulate whole new forms of transaction processing, are emerging. All pretty good stuff. But control of the industry, measured by consolidation, skills, and innovation, is shifting. Fewer vendors, commoditization, devalued skill sets, and modest innovation will combine to change the industry in ways hard to imagine today. Plan for IT.

LEADERSHIP, LIKEABILITY, AND LIFE

Ideas are like viruses: they multiply no matter how hard we try to stop them. For decades I've wondered why there are so many books on management and leadership. I just searched www.amazon.com and found no less than 500,000 links. I then Googled "Leadership Books" and turned up 120,000,000. How can there be so much wisdom on one subject? Does "leadership" change completely every week or so? That might account for all of the "new" thinking about management and leadership.

Or do we just have no idea what leadership is, how to develop it, or how to evaluate it. This might explain why we keep asking the same old questions about leadership, management, and people. The most recent profundity is that people like to work with likeable people even if the nice people don't know very much or produce anything of much value. Isn't this insight what explains how politicians get elected? How movie stars become movie stars? How celebrity CEOs become CEOs?

The book, *The Likeability Factor*, by Tim Sanders and the article in the *Harvard Business Review*, "Competent Jerks & Lovable Fools," by Tiziana Casciaro and Miguel Sousa Lobo, both suggest some really amazingly profound things: people like to work with people they like! Even likeable stupid people like to work with likeable stupid people. Likeable smart people also like to work with other likable smart people. Everybody likes to work with likeable people, even incompetent likeable people. This explains why some likeable politicians can't lead, why some popular actors can't act, and why most celebrity CEOs don't succeed. I don't know about you but this groundbreaking research has thrown me for a loop. Likeable people succeed? Jerks fail? Wow. I have to sit down to absorb the power of this discovery.

I bring all this up because business technology management and leadership are not exempt from the likeability phenomenon. After reading the above two treatises, I sat back and thought about the business technology managers and leaders I've known over the years. How many, I asked myself, were likeable? How many were competent? How many were "lovable fools"? How many were really stupid, nasty, and incompetent? I'm matrix crazy, so I developed Figure 1.3 for us to ponder.

I located the business technology managers and leaders that I've worked with over the years. What do you think I discovered? Well, humbly, I discovered that the likeability scholars are correct (surprise). I found that

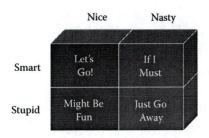

FIGURE 1.3
The people placer.

most of the people were closer to nice and stupid than they were to nice and smart. Stupid? OK, that's probably an exaggeration, but I have to say that I've not been overwhelmed by the rocket science of most technology leaders over the years (technology managers are usually smarter). Leadership, fueled by intelligence, dedication, and passion, is rare.

I can easily identify many technology professionals who were nicer than they were smart. They also seemed to have the knack of being extra nice to the people who promoted them (and to the people who could promote them again). I've also worked with professionals with less than "likeable" personalities. Some of these people were bona fide jerks, but some of the jerks were absolutely brilliant and capable of making extraordinary contributions to their organizations and companies. But, because of their personalities, they were dismissed as "difficult," "obnoxious," or just, well, "unlikeable." Many times in my career I counseled such people with the following advice: "You are absolutely right ... and if you persist, you will be absolutely *dead* right." Lots of careers died at that altar.

All of this might also explain why there are so many consultants. It turns out we need to backfill our staffs with people who are smart, nice, and sometimes nasty (there are no stupid consultants, right?). But, much more important, there's a way to optimize all this (once you've completed the above matrix). Here's what I think you should do:

- Get rid of the stupid nasty people: they serve no purpose.
- Find, retain, and reward smart, nice people—as many as you can.
- Restrict the nice stupid people to roles that exploit their talents, perhaps as communicators, facilitators, and the like, although some pruning here is also necessary. (How many glad-handers do you really need?)

- Work to exploit the contributions that smart, but sometimes nasty, people can make to your projects, programs, and strategies; really smart people are very hard to find.

I think these four steps might actually equal some form of "leadership." Someone should write a book about it. Quick, Google it and see what happens.

DO YOU SPEAK BUSINESS?

Everyone seems to agree that the form and content of "alignment" has forever changed. But all of the conventional arguments about business and technology "silos," the commoditization of IT, and new technology leadership skill sets, although legitimate, miss some important points. Let's look at the evolution of the business technology relationship from "alignment" to "partnership" and three things that must be absolutely true to take the relationship to the next level. These things can be located along continua that you can use to determine how sophisticated your alignment-to-partnership strategy really is. Remember, however, that some targets of "partnership" may not always be open to your affections.

Figure 1.4 identifies three paths in the alignment-to-partnership journey. We have to appreciate business pain and pleasure, we have to become more than just credible, and we have to define business value around

FIGURE 1.4
Paths to business technology partnership.

strategy. If you understand these paths, you can redefine the business technology relationship; I mean *really* redefine the relationship.

Pain → Pleasure

Let's assume that you understand where the business feels pain and how it would define pleasure. Remember that the business expects technology to reduce its pain, defined, of course, around cost reduction. But it's more than that. Business managers worry about their supply chains, their competitors, their manufacturing, distribution, and, of course, their margins. The technology agenda needs to speak directly to their pain points, which when relieved can become the sources of wide and deep pleasure. If you become a dispenser of pleasure as you reduce pain, your credibility will rise, which will reveal the second path to business technology partnership. Put another way, if you help specific individuals make significantly more money, they will love you.

Credibility → Influence

It's hoped that you're credible. It's hoped that when technologists walk into a room the business managers don't run for cover or, worse, attack them mercilessly for their sins (network crashes, website debacles, you know the drill). Nirvana here is influence, defined in terms of how the business thinks about how and where technology can help. Does the business respect you enough to confide in you, to commiserate with you, to invite you to brainstorm about its strategy? With whom do you drink beer?

Operations → Strategy

If you're influential, you can shape both operations and strategy. If you get operations straightened out, you can spend most of your time with your new partners thinking about competitive advantages, revenues, and profitability.

THREE EASY FIRST STEPS

The partnership described here can be engineered by creative, proactive, and motivated business technology professionals. Here are three steps you can take tomorrow:

- Step 1: Make a list of the things that cause your business partners pain, and then rank-order them from their perspective, not yours. Think as they do. The more you do the better the list will be. Work with your partners to validate and improve the list. Then spend some time brainstorming about what your business partners think are the really good things that can happen for them once their pain gets relieved. Focus directly on making them organizationally and personally more profitable. Profitability is the ultimate performance metric.

- Step 2: Honestly assess your credibility with the business. If it's high then think about how to become influential. Some tips here include working through your partner's prism and then supporting the execution of your partner's plans. Once a baseline credibility is established, then transition to influencing important operational and strategic processes. But if your credibility is low, then you have to build it up slowly but surely, principally by delivering effective pain relievers. Candidly, some of you can never recover from past failures and will never become "credible" partners with the business. If you fall into that category, move on.

- Step 3: Use your new-found influence to contribute to strategic planning. The best way to do this is to initiate ideas, models, and pilots. Your partner will appreciate your skin in the game. The perfect outcome here is for your partner to rely upon your insight so much that it would be inconceivable for a new strategic initiative to launch without your fingerprints all over it.

So if you achieve this partnership, what do you give up? A little bit of yourself, a little bit of your experience, and a little bit of your credibility with your legacy peers. What? Yes, because true partnership means that some people get a little less of your time and interest than they used to, that you should probably no longer play cards with the data center crowd, and that you'll have to start reading all new trade publications. You might also have to buy some suits.

WHATEVER HAPPENED TO MENTORING, MERITOCRACIES, AND SABBATICALS?

Whatever happened to mentoring? I don't mean the casual bonding that sometimes occurs between newer and older employees, but formal mentoring programs designed to accelerate the company knowledge acquisition and communication process.

When new people come into an organization they should be given a month to find a mentor to not only show them the proverbial ropes but help them plan their careers in the company. Mentors should be assigned to work with new hires for what equates to a day a week, for at least several months. After that, the mentoring should continue for as long as the employee and mentor are with the company, or until the relationship needs to be changed because of the trajectories of either career: a day a month for life sounds about right.

Mentoring is like continuous orientation. It increases the probability of a successful employee/company match and therefore helps with retention and succession. The worst thing that can happen is spending lots of time and money recruiting people who leave before they make any useful contributions to your company because they were lost somewhere in the shuffle. Formal mentoring is good business, and in order to make it work, positive and negative incentives should be used to make the programs viable.

Speaking of incentives, which ones do you use to keep good people? And how do you use them to send the right messages to the people you don't want to keep? There are lots of arguments here. Some think that the quintessential incentive is money, that no matter what else you offer there better be enough cash (in various forms) to please your star performers. There's a lot of wisdom here. People need to buy food, educate their kids, and pay off their homes. One thing's for sure: if you underpay your top performers you will lose them. We can argue forever about how much is enough, but if you don't pay it you'll lose people (to the competitor that has a database of your good people). So you have to find the right number and stay just above it for as long as you want to keep them on the job.

But money's not the only incentive. Evidence suggests that environments that respect their employees and offer them the right learning opportunities keep their employees. Trust results from a mutually respectful and beneficial relationship between employer and employee. Profound, huh? Actually, although we all pay lip service to platitudes like this, they do keep us balanced, especially when meritocracies lose to golf handicaps.* What does this mean?

---

* See "Meritocracy vs. the Golf Culture," *Business Finance*, August 2002, for a great discussion about how the rules for advancement change the higher you go in the organization.

If there's one aspect of a corporate culture that demoralizes employees at all levels it's the perception (which is too frequently reality) that factors other than merit determine rewards. You've seen it and I've seen it. Frat boys, sorority sisters, and golfing buddies who are anything but brilliant get promoted and rich because of who they know, not what they know or how they perform (and let's not forget their hair). When this kind of reward structure exists it infects organizations at all levels. People become cynical, angry, and disenfranchised when they believe that no matter how hard they work, how right they are, or how well they perform, they won't be appropriately rewarded. So what happens when golf handicaps drive wealth creation? Several things: first, given the message that's sent loud and clear to the troops, the get-along-go-along culture will reduce your overall competency to mediocrity. Many of your employees, in other words, will adapt to the rules of the game by which the buddy system plays. They won't rock the boat, think outside the box, or—God forbid—challenge authority, because they understand that if they piss off the ruling boys or gals they'll never get rich. So they begin to spend more time working on their relationships with the ruling elite than with customers, suppliers, or partners. The obvious result here is that business suffers.

Next, the star performers who really want to improve the business, and who are uncomfortable with "good ol' boy/gal" rules, leave your company to work for one of your competitors (who may or may not play by the same rules). Third, the company will eventually collapse under the weight of these rules if they continue to grow in number and complexity or if they spin out of control into what we've recently seen in the form of corporate anarchy, arrogance, and irresponsibility.

Paid sabbaticals? You bet. When key people work really hard for a long time with consistently impressive results, you occasionally need to give them a rest. Is this that complicated? Look at the companies that offer sabbaticals and see what kind of loyalty they generate.

Performance reviews have been around for a long long time. They are some of the most political processes in your company. Some of your employees are so good at gaming reviews that actual performance has little to do with an employee's assessment. In highly political organizations, people spend a lot of time figuring out how to game performance reviews. In meritocracies, people spend time organizing and presenting performance evidence.

How should you do this? First, publish the process and the outcomes, which include promotions, raises, bonuses, new responsibility, demotions, and dismissals. Each year employees should participate in the development of performance objectives that should be used at the end of the year to assess how well the objectives were met. The employee's immediate supervisor along with a two-person "independent" board should be involved in the review. Am I crazy? Am I suggesting that we get people to agree on what they should accomplish during the year and then review their progress? That three people can do this "objectively"? If the culture supports all this, the answer is yes. But if it doesn't, forget about it.

Overall, we spend too much time worrying about people trivia and not nearly enough on how to grow loyal productive people. Think about mentoring, incentives (positive and negative), meritocracy, sabbaticals, and objective performance reviews. When used correctly, they're all great tools.

─────────────

THREE BRANDS FOR THE MILLENNIUM

It's time to plan your next move. The technology industry still supports tons of people; however, spending and hiring trends don't look all that robust. In fact, there are lots of senior technology professionals still looking for work. What's going on? Is the demand for our services fading? Are we becoming obsolete? No, but there's a big change in the works. Put another way, in five years do you think you'll be doing what you do today? I recently asked 25 senior technology managers at a major public company this question and not one of them raised his or her hand.

The distinction between operational and strategic technology is a good place to start planning how to reinvent yourself. Operational technology is what all of the "IT-is-a-commodity" crowd keeps talking about, you know, the argument that IT no longer generates competitive advantage. Strategic technology is where the action is and is likely to stay. But what do these apparently divergent interpretations of the field tell us about career planning? Tom Peters, a well-known management consultant, guru and writer, suggests we think about "personal brands." Good advice, but what brands will sell?

I think there are three broad ones. And all of them focus on solutions, not problems. Operationally, the brand that will sell is optimization. Technology professionals who can sell themselves as practical yet adaptive infrastructure jockeys will always have work. The necessary skills here include the ability to cost-effectively design and support hardware, software, and communications architectures that directly enable business models and processes. Scalability, reliability, interoperability, and all of the other "ilities" are assumed to be part of the skills repertoire that operational professionals will have. The language these professionals will use is not technospeak: it's the language of business.

Make no mistake here. Many of the infrastructure skills that were highly regarded five years ago will not be held in the same esteem five years from now. Lots of infrastructure technology has already been commoditized and outsourced; more will follow. Infrastructure optimization will be about creative commodity management and bulletproof performance.

If you're not happy with the infrastructure brand, how about branding yourself around strategic technology? If you have wide and deep business knowledge, understand how you and your competition make money, and understand the range of back-office, front-office, and Internet applications through which all the customers, transactions, and money pass, then you can become a business technology strategist. But earning one's stripes here requires creativity about how existing and emerging applications can increase market share and profitability. As with the operational brand, the strategic brand is primarily about business, not technology. Business technology strategists sound (and dress) more like consultants than technologists; brand success here requires a lot of finesse.

The third brand that I think will play well in the early twenty-first century is business technology management guru (which, I suspect, is why you're reading this book). Given what we spend on business technology, keeping the books will become more and more important. But the big brand will be about return on investments, vendor management, program management, and performance metrics, among other skills that help companies acquire, deploy, manage, and measure business technology investments. Knowing when and how to outsource, how to craft a partner agreement, and track the impact of investments on profitability and growth will be the kinds of activities that will define your twenty-first-century management brand.

These three brands suggest how you might think about your next move, how to reinvent yourself. How will colleagues describe your special value to the company in five years? What kinds of skills do you think will sell? Which ones are likely to be devalued? Here are some thoughts. Programmers should move from coding to integrating to architecting; database administrators should move from database management to warehousing to mining; back office/front office applications specialists should move from ERP to extensible transaction processing to scenarios that define future business models and processes; and managers should move from asset management and total cost of ownership to portfolio management and strategic ROI.

Finally, all of the brands require some business success staples, including the ability to effectively communicate complicated ideas, to compromise, negotiate, and prioritize, and, one hopes, your personality doesn't need a major overhaul (because all three brands require some degree of savoir faire). Remember you will need skills to operationalize the brands. I talked above about the new era skill sets you will need to excel as well as the evil soft skills that will save you when all else fails.

So which brand do you like? How will you get there? You, your team, and your organization need a plan to (as suggested above) develop new skills and create brands that the professionals can grow.

FINAL THOUGHTS ABOUT PEOPLE

So what have you learned? Real leverage lies in blood, sweat, and tears, not bits, bytes, and gears. Technology management is organic, not digital (or even analog). Just so you don't think there's a lot of profundity here, the same insight applies to all business and, alas, all human transactions that occur in relationships that together comprise "organizations."

You knew this all the time. I just reminded you to think about the unthinkable. I'm also reminding you to weigh the right factors the right way. Sure, servers, SANs, applications, and e-mail clients are all important, but the real leverage lies with the people who decide what to buy, how to buy, and how to use the technology that in the morning seems interesting and essential but by five o'clock is just a pain in the ass because the deployment "team" screwed up the implementation.

All of this requires the clear acknowledgment of the role that human factors play in technology management and the need to formulate strategic and tactical plans to deal with the deranged, narcissistic, incompetent, and nasty people that surround you. I've provided you with no holds barred insights and dark-side survival skills. Now go use them. Or at least assess their possibilities. It's possible that you, your team, your organization, and corporate culture are all beyond help. Yes, it needs to be said that not all situations are fixable. At the same time, there may be opportunities to dramatically fix some problems or to at least begin the repair process.

2

Organization

This chapter examines at how deranged, narcissistic, incompetent, nasty people organize themselves to achieve their personal objectives while cloaked in the corporate mission. Sure they all talk a good game about how significant the company's strategy is, but actually only see the strategy as a means to personal gain and glory. (Of course there are "good guys" out there trying to do the right thing. But they're usually the cogs in a much larger matrix who are pretty satisfied to get paid for an honest day's work. They are—unfortunately—usually not the ones who organize, decide, and lead.)

Many of our technology organizations work perfectly, if this were 1985. We still insist on coupling everything and avoiding strategic performance metrics (because no one really knows what they look like). We've been through a lot of governance models: people have actually written entire books about governance models. What about our organizational processes? Do they work? How should they be improved? What's really going on in the front office?

Can you organize to exploit some of the new technologies? Obviously, as long as they work and can be matched to meaningful problems, you can organize them. There are also some unique approaches we can take to business technology partnering. There are some new organizational structures that make it easier for technologists to communicate with business managers and executives. We look at some of them. Organizational effectiveness occurs in spite of the human factor. The best we can do is organize in ways that don't make things worse. We talk about that simple objective here. We end this chapter with some clear messages to the technology department and to "management," as well as some guidelines for creating organizations that work.

"I WANT A DIVORCE"

For many CIOs, infrastructure is the essence of their existence. Truth be told, they are chief infrastructure officers, not chief information officers. They spend their days and nights keeping the lights on and running the engine. Many of them do it very well. The smart ones exploit commoditization trends, best practices, and, especially these days, deep discounts in the provisioning of computing and communications gear. CIOs are under pressure today to reduce their budgets even more than they have over the past few years. Lean and mean is taking on a whole new meaning.

But infrastructure is easier to acquire, deploy, and support than strategic technology. Does anyone want to argue that it's easier to upgrade desktops than implement a CRM application? Infrastructure is more predictable and therefore manageable: we understand infrastructure performance metrics much better than strategic technology metrics (if we understand strategic performance metrics at all, which we don't).

Strategic technology that touches customers and suppliers has always been more challenging than operational technology. Life cycles are longer and project scope creep is bigger with strategic technology projects. Expectations are higher as well. Although everyone thinks that e-mail should be bulletproof, they also believe that CRM and business intelligence (BI) applications should transform business processes and instantly spike revenue. The difference is that e-mail *can* be bulletproof, whereas CRM, BI, and similar applications are far from perfect and, in fact, are often pretty lame.

I have thought about the dichotomy for decades. (I realize this means that I have a flat learning curve: if I've been thinking about it for so long then why haven't I solved the problem? You know the answer: people). Infrastructure is completely different from technology intended to transform or improve business processes. Ah, the world of servers, desktops, and networks. I can actually touch them, fondle them if I like. But where are my data on that nasty customer and how do they help me turn an adversarial relationship into a productive partnership? Two different worlds, two different sets of expectations, two different tool sets, two different skill sets: everything's different in these two worlds. So why have they lived together for so long?

One explanation is precedent. Operational and strategic technologies have lived together for a long time, from the "beginning" in fact. But that partnership has always been lopsided: the overwhelming percentage of technology has, since the beginning of technology time, been operational, not strategic. Sure, companies (and their vendors) talk a good game about strategic value but the fact is that the action has mostly been about operational cost effectiveness. This explains the other reason why operational and strategic technologies have lived together for so long: there's hardly any real strategic technology out there.

But it's the twenty-first century and strategic technology is real and robust, or at least it's getting there. Operational technology has actually never been in better shape. Through technologies such as virtualization and voiceover IP, it's never been easier, faster, or cheaper to provision infrastructure services. (Chief infrastructure officers, if they're smart and competent, have plenty of time for golf. In fact, go online to check the handicaps and numbers of rounds played by your favorite CIOs, CFOs, COOs, and CEOs. It's fun to see just how many rounds of golf they sneak in every year as they complain about working too hard.) Although far from perfect and decades from commoditization, strategic technology has also never been in better shape. Maybe it's time for a divorce. Actually, there are no maybes about IT.

Yes, a real divorce. Operational and strategic technology should file (I guess with the high priests of corporate governance) for a divorce. The call here is not for an annulment (they did actually live together and have lots of children), but for an amicable divorce between two parties who, after more than 40 years of a generally good marriage, no longer have anything in common. After the divorce is granted, they should live in different places, report to different people, and be judged for how they achieve a totally different set of accomplishments.

So let's talk post divorce. First, let's define some terms. Operational technology includes the computing and communications infrastructure—the devices, networks, storage, applications support, security, backup, and recovery—that keeps the engine running. It's where the most commoditization has occurred and where best practices, performance metrics, and SLAs are well understood. Strategic technology, on the other hand, is sloppier. The metrics and best practices here are relatively immature.

The focus of strategic technology is on business requirements, business processes, analytics, innovation, customers, and the applications that differentiate the business in the marketplace. As you can see, one is from deep outer space and one is in close orbit. Of huge importance are the differences in skills and competencies necessary to optimize each technology.

FIGURE 2.1
Strategic and operational technology bound by architecture.

In fact, everything's different; they don't even dress alike. Figures 2.1 through 2.3 explain it all pretty well.

All of that said, what should we do with the ex-spouses? Operational technology should be layered under the COO or CAO. (I am not a fan, even though I'm layering operational technology, of any technology reporting to CFOs, who see the world as just one big luxury spending

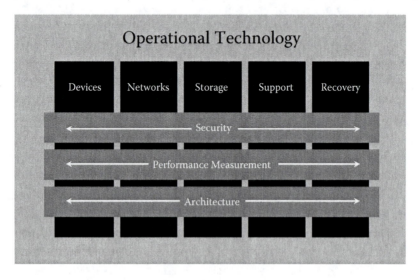

FIGURE 2.2
Operational technology.

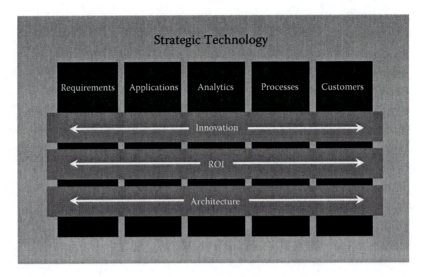

FIGURE 2.3
Strategic technology.

spree that they are biologically wired to stop.) Operational technology is a shared service funded by the enterprise with the lines of business taxed to keep the lights on. A chief infrastructure officer can run operational technology.

Strategic technology should report to the CEO and the lines of business presidents if the company has multiple LOBs. It should have nothing to do with operational technology. Strategic technology delivers discretionary projects driven by business metrics that should speak directly or indirectly to revenue generation. Someone from the business should run strategic technology. I'm not sure what the title of that position should be: maybe something like business technology officer or strategic technology officer.

So what do you think? Is it time for a divorce? Each should go where they should be, and the divorce should end forever all of the arguments and religious wars about governance, organizational structure, funding, and management that have consumed enough time, effort, and money over the years to bail out AIG and Citigroup (or not: it's tough to compete with that level of greed, corruption, incompetence, and arrogance).

A final note about competencies and leadership. Operational technologists are let's-get-it-done pocket-protecting professionals who've cut their teeth on data center operations and server farming. Strategic technologists are professionals who know more about business processes than they do network latency, digital security, or storage area networks. Operational and strategic technologists are about as different as Obama and Bush. I cannot for the life of me understand why they didn't divorce 10 years ago.

Take a look at your organizational structure. If your technology organization is primarily operational, then minor organizational surgery is probably all that's necessary. But if you have two bona fide streams of (operational and strategic) work, then you might consider creating two technology organizations run by two senior executives. The organizations should be joined at the architectural hip. There should be governance-defined coordination, but one shouldn't interfere with the other. They do vastly different things and therefore should proceed very differently to achieve success.

NEW GOVERNANCE VERSUS ORGANIZATIONAL TERRORISM

There's a challenge brewing in the trenches. It's tense, yet opportunistic. It's bottom-up and top-down. It's personal and organizational. It's about power and control. It's complicated and potentially very, very nasty. But, ultimately, it's about survival: we will change or we will die. The fight is about whole new governance models versus organizational terrorism. In other words, enterprises need to change or subject themselves to all sorts of maneuvering on the part of business units and technology groups to acquire more autonomy and decision-making authority. The enterprise can get out in front of this inevitable trend or fight what is certainly a losing battle.

I have talked a lot over the years about trends in the industry, about trends in the technologies themselves, as well as trends in the way we acquire, deploy, and support technology. All of these trends scream for a new way of governing ourselves. What will change? What should change? Let's start the debate here.

Driving Trends

What are the drivers of the new governance?

Let's start with where we've been. By and large IT has been about centralization, standardization, and control. We've also been about national versus global sales and growth. We've communicated to our business partners the limits of technology, technology as a cost center, and technology's vulnerabilities especially in the security area. We've invested in this perspective to the point where business executives see technology as an inhibitor, not an enabler. There are still a lot of business–technology adversarial relationships out there due to this perspective, fed by years of nurturing, that sees technology as a necessary evil, not a source of cost-effective enablement or, heaven forbid, a bona fide partnership.

We're also still wary of new technologies and the impact they might have on business models and processes. Surprisingly, technology managers are often the first to sound the alarm, warning us that new technologies are unproven, not secure, and expensive. Business units, on the other hand, are adopting technologies like Web 2.0 and 3.0 technologies in spite of technology's warnings and trepidations.

But all this will change for a variety of reasons. First, technology itself is decentralizing. End users are no longer just passive recipients of digital technology but proactive adopters and even creators of technology. When did all this begin? Probably in the late 1980s when first-generation client–server computing emerged that distributed computing power across the enterprise. When the Internet became a transaction platform the world changed forever, and when the industry gave us integration and interoperability standards it was anyone's game.

The Internet-as-platform, on-demand computing, and technology consumerization trends are all driving challenges to old governance models. Alternative technology delivery models (X-as-a-service models) are further challenging governance, as is the drive to go increasingly global.

> So what should technology organizations do?
> What are legitimate governance expectations?
> Who should control what?

ALL NEW GOVERNANCE MODELS

Let's organize the challenges to the old governance models:

- Assumptions that digital technology may no longer be a core competency
- Changes in enterprise business technology architectures

- Alternative hardware and software delivery models
- The rise of user-managed Web 2.0 technologies
- The rise of the web as a transaction platform
- Globalization

Let's respond to them in order.

Core Competency Challenges

The very notion that, especially, operational technology has fully commoditized challenges governance in several important ways. Many companies are outsourcing their operational technology to down-the-street or off-shore providers. Who manages this effort? It was assumed just a few years ago that the enterprise technology organization would manage all outsourcing efforts, but more recently we're seeing a participatory approach to operational outsourcing where responsibility is shared across enterprise technology and the business units who are the ultimate clients of the outsourcing process. Obviously, the technology organization knows more about technology performance metrics than the business, but business requirements are better understood by business professionals. Sharing outsourcing governance of even operational technology makes sense especially as we globalize (see below for a larger discussion of the globalization challenge). Strategic technology (technology that faces customers and suppliers) should also be cogoverned by technology and the business.

The challenge here is to staff both technology and business with professionals capable of articulating requirements, managing vendor relationships, and tracking performance metrics. This further means that the business should have veto power over outsourcing initiatives, strategic technology, and shared governance over outsourcing of operational technology. This is a change from where we were in the twentieth century, but consistent with the evolution of the business–technology relationship and trends in the commoditization of operational technology.

Enterprise Business Technology Architecture Challenges

Business technology architecture (assuming that we figure out what it actually is) should be more about flexibility, agility, integration, interoperability, and security than rigorous standards around specific business processes or enterprise applications. This means that companies should select directions and principles rather than one or two specific applications to which everyone must subscribe. Principle-versus-application standardization is an important distinction. As we move more toward service-oriented and event-driven architectures (SOA/EDA), it's easier to standardize on SOA/EDA than on the latest application release from specific vendors.

Governance here should be about SOA compliance, not specific applications. If business units want to deploy applications that will enable their business processes they must comply with the overarching architecture of the company. This frees business units to deploy the applications they need while remaining compliant with the company's overall architectural direction. This represents a change from the twentieth century, expanding the notion of governance from applications to architectures.

Alternative Hardware and Software Delivery Model Challenges

Renting (versus buying and installing) software calls for new governance models. Vendor management will emerge as a core competency for many companies. Service-level agreements (SLAs) must be managed for performance; business units and central IT both have roles to play here. Similarly, renting hardware will emerge as a viable alternative to building and maintaining huge server farms. This trend will challenge governance as well, requiring cooperation between business and technology units because "control" will now involve a third party committed to providing support to the whole company, not just central IT.

Which devices should be selected for personal productivity and management? Smart phones are more than enough for many employees. Which applications—now easily downloadable onto smart phones (aka thin clients)—are "approved" and which are "forbidden"? How do we "police" employees who love to shop in "app stores"? We don't. Again, because of the general trend toward decentralization and the distribution of computing power across and beyond the corporate firewalls, we have to rethink control, authority, and governance: can anyone download anything from the web? Who manages the app store? The solution may be in flexibility with central IT "owning" the due diligence process after business users target specific applications they want to download and use only to make sure that there's nothing in the application that will compromise any aspect of the technology infrastructure or architecture. The net result of all this is a new freedom by professionals to manage their personal productivity with a customized suite of applications they download and use on a daily basis. Note that this governance policy needs to be implemented quickly, because access to increasingly well-stocked app stores will increase dramatically over time. There is no way to control the adoption of easily accessed inexpensive applications.

User-Managed Web 2.0 Technology Challenges

Consumerization has changed the way we introduce technology. Technology adoption actually occurs before employees enter the building. Web 2.0 technologies (wikis, blogs, podcasts, RSS filters, virtual worlds, crowdsourcing, mashups, folksonomies, and social networks) are making their way into companies at an incredible pace. Who's controlling this process? Corporate technology departments are struggling to keep up with the use of these tools by employees, customers, and suppliers. Mashups are the creation of pieces spread out all over the place, that is, inside and outside the corporate firewall. Who controls the APIs, components, and widgets that mash into new applications? How do you prevent blogs and wikis from springing up on an employee's laptop?

Trying to control Web 2.0 technologies is like trying to eliminate global terrorism. But unlike terrorism, which we really need to try to eliminate, we should try to proactively optimize Web 2.0 technologies for the good of the business. For example, business cases for wikis, blogs, podcasts, RSS filters, and other content creation/collaboration tools, should emphasize impact more than cost, risk, and control, because costs tend to be lower and risks tend to be spread across corporation organizations.

The governance around all this requires you to distribute authority around creators and gatekeepers. The central IT organization should, however, maintain control over the components, APIs, and widgets used to create new applications via an internal repository of clean approved components, APIs, and widgets. As long as IT stays current with its evaluation and acceptance process, business professionals can create the mashups and other applications they need. Yes, I realize that this represents a huge change from where we were in the twentieth century, but it's a change that we must embrace, or risk all-out war with the very clients IT needs to enable.

Web Transaction Platform Challenges

Remember when we used to talk about how eBusiness would revolutionize commerce? Well, the distinction between business and eBusiness is gone. web technologies have obliterated the distinction. Now we think of the web as an internal and external transaction-processing platform. Some applications live inside the firewall but extend to the web. Some live only on the web. Some cooperate with other applications both inside and outside corporate firewalls.

Web-based applications represent a challenge to old governance models. They are built quickly and deployed almost instantly. Changes to existing transaction-oriented web sites are immediate. Who governs all this? If a company wants to roll out revised global pricing, does it need to go through corporate IT? Of course not; we crossed that authority chasm a while ago when we invested in user-controlled rule engines and other technologies intended to support real-time decision making. New applications are designed and developed by internal professionals and, increasingly, by outside developers accountable to the business. Application development, rapid application development, and all varieties of web-based applications can no longer be governed by corporate IT except, as suggested above, at the architectural level (which should remain within the control of the technology organization). Yes, this is a change from the past, but the prominence of the web as the emerging dominant transaction platform has changed everything.

Globalization Challenges

Globalization, which I talk about in more detail later in this chapter, is a major driver of new governance models. As more and more companies struggle to increase their global market share, they must adjust the authority they exercise over the business units they want to grow. Decentralization is necessary to enable agile decision making: business units expanding across the globe need the authority to make local and regional decisions. Extending corporate IT from headquarters around the world infrequently makes sense. Servicing an army of ex-pats is expensive and inhibiting. Local talent, local providers, and local/regional/country support make sense as companies build sustainable footprints around the world.

Organizational Implications

All of this calls for new organizational structures. "Headquarters" needs to decentralize. Standards need to become architectural and procedural. CIOs and CTOs need to focus on infrastructure optimization, alternative technology delivery models, architecture, and not much else. The business needs to focus on requirements, application development (within architectural standards), and the deployment of fast/cheap technologies such as Web 2.0 technologies. If we don't adjust our governance then the business technology partnership we've developed will collapse. Terrorism? Probably not, but there will be major pushback from the businesses that want to move quickly and cheaply. If central IT organizations provide roadblocks to these operating principles, there will be hell to pay. Enterprise technology organizations need to rethink how they govern and redistribute power, authority, and control throughout the organization. This is the end-state of the business technology alignment we've been pursuing for decades.

WHY YOU NEED A BUSINESS TECHNOLOGY MANAGEMENT OFFICE

There are a lot of changes going on, changes more profound than the changes the Internet introduced in the 1990s. Now we're wrestling with software-as-a-service, Web 2.0, thin clients, service-oriented architecture, virtualization, BPO and IT outsourcing, always-on connectivity and the mobility it enables, and a general movement toward metrics that speak directly to the business value of technology.

Yes, there's a lot of commoditization in our world and much of it has affected our technology delivery strategies and the role that technology plays in many companies. We still have cost centers, but everyone's now searching for profit centers. Can IT be both?

The relationship between business and technology has never been more center stage than it is today. Technologists must learn more about the business than ever before; business managers and executives need to understand technology's potential. Technologists need to speak the language of business and avoid nerdy references to bits, bytes, and lights. Projects need to be the result of rigorous business case analysis and then managed predictably and professionally. Standards, architecture, and planning also need to be improved to deliver more value to the business.

So what does all this have to do with the reorganization of IT? A lot. The world is shifting away from computing and communications infrastructure and even mainstream business applications toward the business value of technology managed by a set of professionals with relatively new relationship skills, all as suggested in Figure 2.4.

The center of gravity in this new world is the business technology management office (BTMO), which owns all project demand, prioritization, and execution management. The actual work continues to occur in the infrastructure and applications groups; however, the BTMO is the face of technology to the business. Figure 2.4 suggests you do the following:

- Create a business technology management office responsible for all work requests and the prioritization of all work; integrate a project management office (PMO) into the BTMO, because project management is critical to success; increase the number of business relationship managers (BRMs) so they may be devoted full-time to the businesses; add dotted line responsibility from all business analysts (BAs) to the BTMO; add architecture and standards to the group; position the BTMO as the face of IT for the business; develop a work-flow roadmap that describes the initiation through the execution and audit processes; communicate to the company that the BTMO will be given authority over all work requests; modify the governance process to accommodate the new role of the newly expanded BTMO; continuously communicate the changes to the technology and businesses; seek and solidify buy-in and support from senior management for the suggested organizational changes.
- Rigorously segment work according to value/cost/risk with tight reference to profitable growth project priorities.
- Deepen requirements modeling/requirements documentation/ requirements traceability around work requests and work processing.
- Implement "CRM for BRM" so that BRMs can build business and stakeholder profiles, problem matrices, other relationship-focused data, and, especially, business and personal performance metrics.
- Develop a portfolio of (IT) solutions for use by the IT and business communities; specify the repertoire of solutions in a language and form that the business can understand and evaluate; begin the work

request process, scoping, and vision, with a visit to the portfolio to optimize the application of existing solutions.

- Implement some form of allocation/accounting model for project management and resources based on projected business/service growth and profitability.
- Develop a standard engagement model for interacting with the business.
- Develop an "About the Business" boot camp customized for BRMs, PMOs, and BAs.
- Build ongoing profiles of the business and especially business and personal performance metrics; build opportunity/challenges/best practices/impact matrices for the business.
- Invest in knowledge management for improved BRMs to include business profiles, performance metrics, solutions, training, projects, audits, and the like; assign a team to pull together existing materials that might populate the knowledge base.
- Expand an "About the Business" approach to deepen the technology organization's understanding of business models, processes, threats, opportunities, and so on.
- Develop an "About Technology" program for the business from brief overviews to more in-depth explanations of how technology works at the company for both (business and technology) audiences.

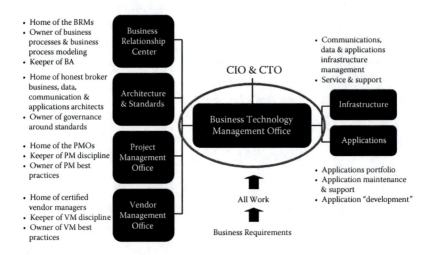

FIGURE 2.4
The new center of gravity.

- Expand communication with the business about IT's capabilities and IT's best practices for optimizing technology: invest in the "marketing" of IT.
- Certify a subset of BRMs as professional internal consultants; incentivize these consultants to mentor professionals in the company.
- Provide skills training for time management, negotiation, knowledge management, meeting management, and oral/written communications for BRMs, PMOs, VMOs, and BAs.
- Provide standardized skills training to BRMs, PMOs, VMOs, and BAs.
- Provide training to improve and extend decision-making skills throughout the organization to promote efficiencies.
- Identify a set of modeling, analysis, and decision-making tools to facilitate communication with the businesses, prioritization of work, and reporting, such as Michael Porter's Five Forces strategy model, multicriteria decision making, and systems dynamics "what-if" analysis tools; identify a suite of modeling tools and techniques that become standard tools and techniques for the BTMO.
- Offer skills training at two levels: awareness training and deep training, where the former becomes a gate for the latter for those especially qualified and motivated.
- Develop vendor management skills, methods, tools, and templates to optimize sourcing decisions.

The reorganization of technology around a business technology management office is radical yet consistent with the trajectory of business technology partnership and optimization. By its very definition, the BTMO changes the emphasis from technology infrastructure and mainstream business applications to a business technology partnership designed to enable operational and especially strategic business models and processes. It also rearranges the pieces that many current IT organizations have spread out all over the place. The integration of the PMO and VMO into the BMTO signals coordination among these important functions. The business relationship center (BRC), where the BRMs and BAs sit, becomes a repository of solutions, relationships, business profiles, and skills to improve the business technology partnership.

Who "loses" in this reorganization? The power once held by infrastructure and applications is reduced in this model. But although infrastructure and applications continue to be about as important as any enabling function in every company, the relative importance of these groups is shrinking in favor of activities and functions designed to make the business technology relationship as seamless as possible.

When all's said and done, IT organizations need to tilt toward the businesses they support, toward the language of business, to business performance metrics, and to growing professionals capable of understanding, supporting, and even commiserating with the business. The reorganization suggested here will help align technology to the business and begin the inevitable shift of power from infrastructure and applications to relationships, consulting, and (project, program, and vendor) management. Regardless of how technologists feel about this trend, it is inevitable: technology management will supersede technology implementation and support. Of course, technology will always need to be implemented and supported but where and how it occurs is likely to leave the enterprise, whereas technology optimization through best practices management will be with us for decades and decades to come. Maybe, just maybe, technology will make its way from a cost center to a profit center. At least that's the plan. But remember in order to get there, you'll need to feed the personal financial vested interests of the "deciders."

WHAT TO DO WHEN THE REGIONS REBEL

Recognizing that Tom Friedman's book *The World is Flat* has been out for years, many of you are still struggling with how to extend our computing and communications infrastructures and architectures around the world, away from the proverbial "home office."

Globalization is as much a political challenge as it is a technical one. Not in the sense of what the host government's politics are all about (although that's sometimes important), but about internal corporate politics, governance, and culture (and the jerks that just cannot give up control for fear of losing part of their bonuses). In fact, global IT success is more defined around how we behave as it is around the technology we buy, deploy, and support. In other words, it's like home all over again. So here we go.

You work at a company with multiple lines of business that increasingly finds its revenue coming from places other than where the home office is. Your longer-term strategy is to optimize these revenue streams. You need to figure out how to extend your infrastructure and architecture to the hinterlands. Here are 10 thoughts. Note that they're not presented here as one-size-fits-all; in fact, globalization is the antithesis of convention or standardization, or at least that's the argument you should strongly consider.

1. The first job is to distinguish between communications infrastructure and applications architecture. It may be possible to keep everyone on your messaging platform regardless of where everyone works. Here's where Friedman was right. Some applications should also extend to wherever they need to be, especially ERP and personal productivity applications (although perhaps not in their fullest versions; see number 3). Network and systems management applications should also extend easily and cost-effectively. But things get real fuzzy when it comes to business applications that are not part of the infrastructure. Here you might want to decentralize application standardization and support and allow the hinter businesses to acquire, deploy, and support applications of their choice. You should standardize on architecture, such as service-oriented, architecture-based standards, but if there's too much blowback from even this degree of control, you should redefine governance as a retreat from the control days long gone.

2. Consider open-source software for the troops on global patrol. In fact, global rollout of open-source software can be viewed as a home office pilot intended to vet the strengths and weaknesses of open-source solutions (or at least this is how it might be sold to both the outposts and home office). Think about it: if you're starting a new business in Asia, for example, you might want to rethink the whole acquisition/deployment/support process. You might learn a lot about open-source software from the outposts; so much, in fact, that you might even consider open-source adoption at home. Remember that start-ups are looking closely at open-source applications and are avoiding proprietary applications wherever they can. Does globalization represent start-up-like opportunities? Sure.

3. Identify "lite" versions of infrastructure and business applications. Do you really need all of those ERP modules in Latin America or Asia or North America? Probably not, so consider renting the functionality that you need. Here again the outposts can provide pilot opportunities for alternative technology delivery models such as software-as-a-service (SaaS). The fastest and cheapest way to deploy the software you need is to pay-by-the-drink versus installing, and then extending, complicated enterprise platforms all over the world.

(As an aside, would you know how to do this if you decided to do it?) At first blush you may think that the smartest thing to do is extend an existing investment as far as you can, but it may be that you'd be better served by not only avoiding the global extension of business applications but planning to decommission them altogether as you rethink your overall upgrade and migration strategies. Yes, I am strongly suggesting that you may want to start weaning yourself from your installed enterprise applications in favor of some alternative acquisition and delivery models, such as SaaS.

4. Consider local technology support instead of tasking your home office support to extend to Asia, Latin America, Europe, North America, Central America, or anywhere else you need to go. Sure, the usual suspects have long arms and legs, but many home office vendors stay stateside, and if you task IBM, Unisys, Accenture, PWC, or EDS to support you globally, you may end up paying more because of their overhead and labor structures (unless you aggressively exploit their indigenous teams through tough contract negotiations). They may also have holes in their support, especially if you veer too far from home office "standards." They may be simply unable to support unfamiliar indigenous applications.

5. Only deploy applications that are compliant with local/national/ regional regulations rather than customizing noncompliant applications. In the financial services industry, for example, not all systems are compliant with some country regulations. Local support will point you to "certified" applications to run your business. Make sure that the whole applications suite "works" for the country and region in which you find yourself.

6. Consider loosening the control on what the outposts do (and don't do). This will be tough because you may have worked hard to define and implement the governance you have in place today, governance that probably speaks directly to control through enterprise standards, among other mechanisms. But do all of these mechanisms apply globally? Consider revisiting governance and relaxing some of the "rules" that may not apply to specific countries and regions. This will be hard for you to do inasmuch as the last 30 years of technology management have been about control, standardization, governance, due diligence, and, ultimately, a best practices discipline that has given the field credibility and respect. But it may be that control has limits and that we need to rethink the hammers we use to influence

behavior. Remember that if local/regional/national outposts have pure profit-and-loss (P&L) responsibility, then enterprise controls will be challenged at every turn. Maybe it makes sense to get out in front of this debate.

7. Consider increasing the funding for discretionary projects designed to help the country and region in which the business is operating. These increases should be especially large in high-revenue-growth countries and regions, inasmuch as in this case the mother ship is betting big on global growth. Put another way, it makes sense to segment investments by country, region, and revenue growth, with most of the money going to the high-growth countries and regions. Yes, this is a zero-sum game, so the more money that goes to specific high-growth global outposts the less there will be for everyone else. But doesn't that investment strategy make sense? Do not hold on to egalitarian funding strategies because they feel "fair." Globalization represents an opportunity to redistribute corporate wealth.

8. Consider changing the organizational structure to create mini-IT organizations regionally rather than extensions of home office structures. This is the ultimate decentralization strategy, and will keep your professionals off the phone late at night or early in the morning from "checking in" 24/7. Let them breathe a little, but hold them accountable to specific performance metrics.

9. Grow people regionally rather than shipping them from the home office to spend tours of duty around the world. The day IT arrives in a country or region is the day the in-country succession plan should begin.

10. Finally, change the way the bills are paid. The hinterlands should have their own budgets consistent with the applications and organizational decentralization discussed above. Although they can continue to pay for the infrastructure they use, they should have the ability to expense technology initiatives as they see fit with a budget that's accountable to the line of business they support. If a regional shared service model is adopted because multiple lines of business are operating in the same country or region, then that too should have budget flexibility independent (with the exception of shared infrastructure) of the home office's budgeting processes.

These are some thoughts about how to extend technology without triggering a hundred turf wars about who owns what, who controls what, and, ultimately, who's accountable to whom. One thing is for sure. If companies empower lines of business to conquer specific countries or regions to produce profitable growth—and incentivize them to do so—then these lines of business will push for the autonomy they believe they need to succeed. This will, in turn, pull technology in the same direction: more autonomy, less enterprise control, and more financial freedom. It's time to rethink the rules around the globalization of technology. Get on with IT.

PROCESSES, CLEAR AND MESSY

It's not the technology, it's the processes. Processes are good, bad, ugly, or indifferent depending on how well, or poorly, you incentivize their efficacy. Let me repeat: it's not the technology. In fact, among the triumvirate of people, process, and technology, technology is the least likely cause of failure. Then comes people. But there's huge leverage in the processes we anoint as our problem-solving saviors. Many of these processes literally make people crazy.

Processes are political. They are intended to govern behavior. Sometimes the processes are the result of a democratic procedure to determine which processes make the most sense, that is, with which ones we think we can live. Other times they're the result of a dictatorial organization's desire to control policies and procedures. Some companies have hybrid processes: some are inviolate, some are ill-defined, and some are actually negotiable. But where do they come from? How are they protected? How are they optimized?

Process World

We love processes; we hate processes. We love them because they make us feel professional, like grownups who pretend to know what they're doing, and because they define the steps we hope will yield meaningful results. Processes are often not about the destination but more often about the journey. Processes are the result of someone's thinking about how to accomplish something and the deconstruction of the steps that when taken sequentially yield value. We hate processes because they slow us down, make us rethink what our instincts are telling us, and essentially require us to kneel at the altar of bureaucrats. After all, doesn't father know best?

There are processes for everything. There are order-to-cash processes, manufacturing processes, distribution processes, sales processes, supply chain processes, marketing processes, eBusiness processes, data processes, training processes, application development processes, succession planning processes, change management processes, maintenance processes, and even process control processes, among too many others to list here. The world is awash in processes.

Processes come in all sizes, shapes, and forms. They are defined and managed by all sorts of people within your organization. Part of the challenge is process management across functional areas. In technology, for example, there are infrastructure processes, communications processes, and applications processes. There are also project management processes. Process synchronization is a problem for process-oriented organizations, especially when processes clash. In order to avoid process conflict, process-oriented cultures should try to standardize as many processes as they can.

Most processes are codified and "approved." Or at least they should be. No kidding, there needs to be a process reference book that skeptics can consult when their best instincts are offended. Process handbooks are essentially internal service-level agreements. Processes can be blogged and wikis can be used to evolve processes over time. Processes should be online and accessible to everyone. They should be transparent: the source of the process and its history should be available to anyone who wants to understand where the process came from and how it has changed over time.

Processes are also described in varying levels of detail. Some are extremely well described down to the most diagnostic detail. There are the ones that should go on the to-be-automated list. Organizations that prefer relatively vague process descriptions are protecting their use of ambiguity, where ambiguity can be their friend when the occasion arises. These organizations are process players, not doers. Organizations that prefer detailed process descriptions want their processes to truly govern behavior.

Process management is time intensive. Processes should be reviewed at least annually. Process teams should be assigned ownership; corporate governance must embrace all of the approved processes. But these teams should only meet in conference rooms with no chairs. Otherwise they'll become process bureaucrats who help no one but themselves.

There should be an exceptions management process that enables professionals to challenge processes in the context of problems that arguably extend beyond the relevance of approved processes. The larger governance framework should define what happens when a process is challenged or an exception is requested.

Good processes that get ignored with impunity undermine organizational effectiveness. (Wow, did I actually say that?) Professionals will not respect stupid processes or processes that have no governance clout. Such processes sit out there for everyone to ignore and mock: not a good thing because it calls the credibility of the entire organization into question. Why do you even have processes on the books if no one pays any attention to them? Be very careful with this dimension of the process world. Your employees will find broken processes, and complain about them, as fast as heat-seeking missiles find infernos. If I have heard this once I have heard it a thousand times: "Yeah, we have all those processes but no one actually follows them; we short circuit anything that takes time or costs money."

Process Control

Some years ago General Motors (GM) created process information officers (PIOs) to manage and ultimately control common processes across business units. These process officers were empowered to define, manage, and assess processes across the globe. The essence of the new officers' mission was to assure that the right processes were applied the right way at the right time. Because these process officers reported to the global GM CIO they also represented some governance clout that spoke to centralization and decentralization. The process officers were horizontally focused and part of the centralized enterprise technology organization. There were five PIOs for (1) supply chain processes, (2) product development processes, (3) production processes, (4) customer experience processes, and (5) business services processes. Because there were business unit CIOs that reported to their business unit directors, the enterprise CIO required the PIOs to report to the enterprise and not the business units. This provided horizontal control on what otherwise were relatively independent business unit CIOs. Clever, huh? Nothing more than a power grab (which worked until GM itself melted down and the internal technology enemies list shrunk to a handful of Rick Wagoner's BFF executives who were distracted by threats to their own careers).

Other controls are anchored in broader governance that requires organizations to adhere to predefined steps to achieve specific goals. All processes taken together, along with other organizational "rules," define corporate governance. Still other controls are delegated to outsourcers empowered to enforce process standards. Handing over processes to vendors is an interesting strategy for achieving compliance. It's especially useful to weakly governed organizations that may have tried just about everything to achieve compliance, but have ultimately failed. Outsourcers tie process control to cost where process exceptions may be occasionally granted but always cost a whole lot more.

Process ownership extends from organizational structures. Decentralized organizations will distribute process ownership and control to the business units. Centralized organizations retain ownership over everything.

Process Improvement

Processes are living artifacts. They're meant to be changed over time. These days they're the target of process improvement specialists (who masquerade under any number of quality improvement aliases [like Black Belts]). The business process management (BPM) discipline is focused squarely on mapping and improving processes. BPM tools abound as do the consultants out there who can help you model and improve processes.

I'm a huge fan of BPM and BPM tools. I like them because they link what technologists do to what matters to business partners. I also like them because they facilitate "what-if" sensitivity analyses that enable assumptions to be challenged. I also like the ones that have interactive graphic displays customizable for managers and executives who need to be entertained as well as engaged. I actually believe that BPM should become a core competency for technology organizations (and I no longer believe in much at all).

Process Incentives

Processes are living political artifacts. We use them to define steps that might otherwise be challenged. We use them to remove ambiguity from operations. But how do we get everyone to follow processes? Positive incentives always work better than negative ones. The best positive incentives are the ones that service personal and business financial metrics. To put it bluntly, personal performance metrics are about personal financial rewards: cash, bonuses, stock grants, stock options, and so on. Business performance metrics focus on sales, cost controls, and profitability, among others. The best metrics, of course, are the ones that satisfy both objectives: cash and profitable revenue.

Another class of personal performance metrics worth noting is the extent to which a successful process makes someone a hero. The perfect metric here makes someone a hero who eventually gets promoted because of all of the processes that served everyone— and the organization—so well. Other incentives are anchored in the politics and culture of the organization. If compliance is expected and conformity is high, then the reward lies in the acceptance of the process for what it is. If, on the other hand, compliance is optional, then negative incentives may be necessary to get people to do what they should do.

Takeaways

So what have we learned here? I hate when managers hide behind obsolete processes just to get their own way. I also hate processes that no longer apply to vastly changed business models. Finally, I hate processes designed to slow things down. I realize that processes can contribute to business success through consistency and repeatability, but I also realize that sub-optimal processes can stifle creativity and productivity.

I like processes that keep us all honest and especially the ones that amplify transparency. I also like processes that adapt to a world that changes frequently and without notice. Processes that logically integrate into flexible governance models are also good.

Watch your processes and your process controllers. Make sure that they do what they're supposed to do, and nothing more (or less). Also make sure that your processes are credible. In order for them to be effective, they have to be implemented by professionals who respect their value.

THE SUBTLE, SUBLIME, AND NEFARIOUS (OR, WATCH YOUR BACK)

So maybe it's just the people I hang around with, or maybe it's just me, but my radar about what's being said between the lines is getting keener and keener. Communications professionals have long sensitized us to the elements of effective communication, which always includes insight and attention to the "sender," the "message," the "channel," and the "receiver." The message is the focus here. There are often clear and not-so-clear parts of business technology messages. It's important for your survival, especially these days, to fully understand what's said and what goes unspoken. Sometimes it's what's not actually said that's the most important part of the message.

So here's an attempt to increase our sensitivity to the discussions swirling around us. It's an attempt to ferret out purpose and meaning from glib phrases and talking points. It's like the difference between syntactic and semantic understanding, the difference between what's said versus what's meant. So listen up. Here's what might really be going on in your organization.

Training to Obsolescence

When management stops training, the troops should step back and wonder why, really. Usually they say something about saving money (especially in these times), "We'd love to train everyone on the latest and greatest technologies and technology management processes, but we just don't have the funding right now; we hope to free up some funds for training next year." What's the real message here? Well, of course, it could very well be that there are no funds for training this year. But it might also be that senior management is throwing in the towel, deciding to stop increasing its intellectual capital. If that's the plan, then it sets up an argument some time down the road about just how obsolete the skill sets among the organization's technology professionals have become, skill sets that they undermined by their lack of training investment. The development of talent is taken seriously or it's not: lip service to the importance of people is one thing, but funding is something else altogether. Pay attention to what they fund, not what they say.

Also track general educational benefits at your companies. Many of your organizations will fully or partially reimburse undergraduate and graduate education. A few even support the pursuit of doctoral degrees. If these benefits get reduced or eliminated, management may be sending a clear signal about how it values education and, ultimately, you.

CAPEX versus Expensing

The days of monster CAPEX technology projects are numbered, especially until we emerge from the financial funk the world's in: can you defend a multiyear project with a multiyear payback period with high enterprise license fees and even higher priced consultants? Who's going to launch such a project today?

When organizations move money from CAPEX projects to projects that can be annually expensed they're sending another signal about long-term technology commitments. The beauty of CAPEX projects is that they're destined to live forever, or at least as long as the depreciation schedule. But more important, big CAPEX technology projects represent a technology acquisition strategy that is inherently stable and persistent. Projects that are expensed represent a whole different acquisition and deployment philosophy. When projects are annually expensed, there's a short-term bias built into the investment. There's no depreciation to worry about and therefore no long-term financial commitment to the project.

Of course moving away from CAPEX funding may also represent a desire to move to alternative technology delivery models, such as software-as-a-service, hardware-as-a-service (HaaS), and infrastructure utility services. But as these models are deployed they shift technology finances to a more flexible investment approach that ultimately puts some distance between the technology and the organization it serves. Lock-in is avoided as flexibility grows. Is this always deliberate? No, but it sometimes is. Pay attention to what investment trends and approaches might mean; close attention.

Those Things Are Expensive

One of the new technology delivery models encourages employees to bring their personal computers to work where they will be granted access to corporate networks, databases, applications, and so on. "We will make your machine work here; don't worry; it's our responsibility." Sounds great to some of us who just love our PCs (especially the Mac users among us), and absolutely hate the corporate standard machine. The pilots around this delivery model are insidious plots to eventually deny employees company-purchased PCs. If the numbers are compelling we'll all start hearing arguments like: "Well, if you were a carpenter, I'd expect you to bring your own tools to work." This is the quintessential trade argument which, of course, makes technology professionals tradespersons, which many of them actually are. Be wary of the motive behind these pilots disguised as, "We just want to make you happy," corporate initiatives. The amount of money that companies could save by requiring employees to use their own computers is staggering. Enormous savings usually attract lots of attention, especially in tough times. We're not there yet, but as interoperability architecture standards widen and deepen, supporting multiple machines, operating systems, and architectures will become relatively easy, especially if IT's only responsibility is network access. Imagine how appealing it would be to leave the acquisition, deployment, and break-and-fix world altogether. Help desks may be the next to go as companies replace support with crowd-sourcing models or approaches that place responsibility to being efficient on employees (after all, carpenters don't ask their bosses to fix their tools).

Sourcing

We talk a lot about sourcing in Chapter 4, but there are some clear organizational implications of alternative sourcing models. But be careful about the real message around sourcing. Although outsourcing can be valuable (defined in terms of cost savings and the redefining of a company's core competencies) it can also be a ruse. Sometimes it's a ruse designed to confuse vendors. For example, shops that have long ago standardized on a specific PC brand frequently indicate that they might be willing to unstandardize with a new vendor. Sometimes it's sincere, but often it's just a ruse to keep the incumbent vendor honest. Some of these buyers may actually write and issue an RFP to demonstrate their seriousness about finding an alternative vendor.

Another ruse is the use of outsourcing to implement governance when a company cannot otherwise govern itself. It's fun to watch previously ungoverned lines of business adjust to the outsourcer who tells them that everything is à la carte. "What do you mean it will cost me extra to stray from the company standard?" Better than that: "Well, we'd love to accommodate you, but the vendor tells us that it will cost you a lot more to vary your environment. Can you believe those guys?" Of course, the real message is that "Because we're unable to govern ourselves we've hired these nasty people to govern us. Good luck with them."

Telecommuting's Not for Everyone

In turbulent times companies try to save money in all sorts of ways. One is to reduce operations costs by shutting down offices for a day a week, or sending large numbers of people home to do their work. Sometimes it's about cost savings and sometimes it's about other things. But it's not always what you think. Organizations that are reluctant to send their employees home to work sometimes resist telecommuting because they cannot manage to outcomes, only processes. Many managers have to actually see their employees working. They define productivity and accountability around physical presence. Other managers define productivity around the results of work. Outcome-versus-process management often drives decisions about telecommuting. Some companies will kill telecommuting simply because they cannot figure out how to manage by outcomes. Organizationally, there are major implications to telecommuting. Does the company want to save money by reducing office space? Does it want to phase out selected full-time employees by sending them home to eventually work on a project-by-project basis? Is telecommuting a strategy to increase the number of 1099 employees a company has? Watch your backs here.

Change for Their Own Sake

The mandate for change is everywhere. No one ever takes a stand against positive change, moving forward, or getting things done. But it's important to assess the context in which the mandate expresses itself. When executives champion change, they should immediately be evaluated in the context of the change they're spearheading. How deep is the commitment to change? Are there resources for enabling change? Are they personally committed to change? Will they be there as the changes unfold? Big CAPEX projects with five-year tails designed to change the company championed by 63-year-old CEOs (who must retire at 65) are more about cause than effect. (It's like well-publicized stock buyback plans that result in but a few shares actually being purchased.) The point is that change requires real commitment across a broad set of executives who fund the change without ambiguity. Anything short of this should call the change commitment into question. Big projects and transformational agendas are sometimes real and sometimes something else. When change is declared, check to make sure it's real, sustainable, funded, and smart. One metric is the extent to which a public company publicizes a major project to its customers, employees, and especially its investors. If there's broad publicity around the change it's more likely to sustain itself than if the change agenda is held closely to the vest of a small number of change champions.

These are only some of the things we should watch as we navigate troubled waters. Management is sometimes confused about what to do, but sometimes it engages in sleight of hand, in decisions designed to confuse employees to keep management's options open. In other words, sometimes they deliberately engineer futures quite distinct from their rhetoric. So listen, watch, and react, and be careful out there. We're entering some extremely troubled waters that no one's ever mapped. So what you hear may actually be what to fear.

HAVING IT BOTH WAYS, YOU BASTARDS

We find ourselves in a conundrum: just as technology hands us some powerful new opportunities, the financial markets constrain our ability to exploit them.

What to do?
Have IT both ways.

Here's the short list of how to think about how to exploit the trends defining the industry in the early twenty-first century and how to convince skeptics that the money will really be well spent. (I will turn to the bastards who created all these skeptics after vetting the short list of save money/make money/exploit technology opportunities.)

Save Money Today and Make Money Tomorrow

The marching orders today are to cut technology costs but longer-term the orders will be about cutting costs and generating revenue. There will be clear and consistent pressure placed on technology organizations to perform as both cost centers and profit centers. Prepare for the schizophrenia. Do not throw the baby (profit center) out with the bath water (cost management). Assign someone to whisper in your ear every time you announce that you found another X% to cut that the world does not turn on cost management alone, that this too shall pass, and we'll once again turn to technology to enable profitable growth. That said, of course, there will always be pressure to reduce technology costs. So get used to being all things to all people; it's a permanent state.

Stop Worrying about Devices

It doesn't matter how we get to networks, data, and applications, only how we get there securely and ubiquitously. We buy one device brand instead of another because we get a better deal, not because we think there are significant performance or reliability differences. There aren't. Interoperability is just about complete. Soon it won't matter what device is used to access networks, data, and all forms of media. All content is mobile; all devices are (soon to be) interoperable. Don't build or buy anything that only works in one place (unless you like wearing tool belts). You can save money here, and make money by increasing the productivity of your clients. You should also segment your clients into categories that match them to the devices they actually need, and those they don't. Interoperability means that one size no longer needs to fit all.

Software and Hardware Are Already Services

Only organizations that believe they must absolutely, positively own their data, applications, and infrastructure will persist with the buy/install/develop/customize/support process. Just about everyone else will rent applications over the web. The software-as-a-service model will enable the trend, inasmuch as we'll not only be able to rent standard application packages but we'll also be able to customize applications over the web. You can also rent servers from Amazon, Yahoo, or EMC, among others, for less than a dollar a day. You can rent just about anything from a growing number of vendors. Pilot some of these alternative hardware delivery models against a set of cost/benefit metrics. What the hell are you waiting for?

Open-Source is Safe, Honestly

Open-source software is not competition to proprietary software, it augments it; in fact, within a few years it will begin to replace significant stacks of proprietary software. Will we see the increased adoption of open-source desktop software (to compete with MS Office) and even Linux on the desktop? Will we see the widespread adoption of open-source CRM and database applications? Yes and yes. The major proprietary software vendors will reduce their prices to avert the increased adoption of open-source solutions. It remains to be seen how aggressively they fight, but they have to make some tough decisions here, and soon. Just download Open Office and be done with it (or StarOffice, or GoogleApps, or even Symphony).

There's Gold in Them There Processes

Buy, rent, or activate an existing business process modeling application at your company. Many of you already have access to a BPM module through our larger ERP platforms. There are lots of off-the-shelf packages as well. It makes sense to invest in process modeling training and internal process consulting; BPM expertise should become core to your company. There's leverage (and gold) in designing, simulating, tweaking, and implementing alternative business processes.

WEB 2.0 IS REALLY YOUR FRIEND

The first wave of Web 2.0 applications was met with caution in the enterprise. Neanderthal technology managers saw wikis, blogs, RSS filters, podcasts, mashups, folksonomies, crowdsourcing, and virtual worlds as threats to their governance processes and, ultimately, their control over the technology. The second wave of Web 2.0 applications is turning heads: wikis for training, blogs for customer service, crowdsourcing for innovation, and RSS filters and folksonomies for content management and distribution, among many other creative uses of the technology. This is an opportunity on a silver platter. Take full advantage of it. It's fast and cheap, perfect for the times.

Data without Analytics Are Useless

Many companies underexploit their data. (Of course just as many have problems simply finding and certifying their data.) But the real payoff is what the data tell us about manufacturing, distribution, customers, sales, marketing, and service, among other activities core to the business. The 3:1 rule is in effect here: for every dollar you spend on database management technology you should spend three on analytics. All DBMS investments should be vetted through analytics criteria.

ORGANIZATIONAL SURGERY IS NO LONGER ELECTIVE

Objectively assess your organizational structure and effectiveness. How's it working for you? Who's reporting to whom? Why? And how are they compensated? Bold lines versus dashed lines are tricky. Make it clear who accounts to whom. Do you need a project management office? How about a vendor management office? You need a business relationship center of some kind, and you need to populate the center with kick-ass business relationship managers, the owners of the intersection of business requirements and technology solutions. People assessment is always tough and always political: "What do you mean my brother-in-law is an idiot?" "I guarantee you that my mistress is valuable: stop picking on her!" The economic times provide all the air cover you will ever need to make tough people decisions. Take advantage of the times or wait until the next major downturn. Restructure things to accommodate the new technology and technology delivery models. Do you think that Web 2.0 technology and SaaS/HaaS require different operating and organizational protocols?

Loosen Up

As mentioned previously this is tough for the fascists in your organization who thrive on total control, but decentralization is inevitable, not so much of infrastructure but definitely for applications that increasingly support global activities. Standardization will be around architecture, like service-oriented, architecture-based standards. Local technology support makes sense instead of tasking the home office to extend support to Asia, Latin America, Europe, North America, Central America, or anywhere else you need to go. Consider loosening the control on what the outposts do (and don't do). Consider relaxing some of the rules that apply to specific countries and regions. Control has limits and we need to rethink the hammers we use to influence behavior. Remember that if local/regional/national outposts have pure profit and loss responsibility, then enterprise controls will be challenged at every turn. Maybe it makes sense to run from this debate. Grow people regionally rather than shipping them from the home office to spend tours of duty around the world. I repeat, the day IT arrives in a country or region is the day the in-country succession plan should begin.

It's Getting Cloudy Out There

Small and mid-sized companies have embraced cloud computing for several reasons, including cost, flexibility, and the desire to define operational technology as a minor (if any) part of their core competency. Even some larger companies have taken the plunge (or jumped into the ether) usually in pieces: a little SaaS here, a little HaaS there. One of the major strengths of cloud computing is the freedom it provides companies to think strategically about how they want to leverage technology. Instead of worrying about network latency and server maintenance, companies can focus on innovation, sales, and marketing, among other revenue-generating activities. Picking from a menu is easier than creating one. Scalability is often just a phone call, text message, or e-mail away. The freedom from software maintenance, denial-of-service attacks, viruses, and other operational headaches is a byproduct of cloud computing. Ultimately, cloud computing can save companies 20% to 25% depending, again, on the nature of the infrastructure, the number of users, and the number of applications put to work. Time to plug into the cloud to see what it can do for you.

OK, so times are tough, and, candidly, they will probably get worse. Technology spending will continue to fall. This is not a "normal" recession. We have been mismanaged by an army of greedy bastards who came close to ruining our economy. Sadly, this not only includes those who packaged and repackaged (and repackaged) subprime mortgages, but also the politicians who ignored the problems as they accepted money from any number of contributors interested in their re-election. It also includes the bastards on Wall Street who raped and pillaged the economy before and after the bailout. What a country.

The decrease in technology budgets is one of the many, many outcomes of all this accountability-free incompetence, greed, arrogance, and fraud that describes the recent past. Our industry will suffer for years because of what these bastards did and failed to do. Thank God that the dependency on technology has never been greater, so great, in fact, that no one can walk away from his technology infrastructures and applications and stay in business. The challenge now is to make the right tough decisions in the right way, decisions that have two sides. The first side is about managing through this unprecedented crisis; the second side is about prospering when it finally ends. Technology trends can help with both sides of the equation. New delivery models, for example, can help us save money today and improve our efficiencies tomorrow.

Ending on an optimistic note (!), I've never seen technology trends able to simultaneously save money and make money in the short term and longer term. I've also seldom seem so much willingness to make tough decisions, though this may have something to do with how many houses are on fire.

FIVE HOURS TO INFLUENCE

A CIO friend of mine recently asked me the following question: "If you had five hours to communicate a message to the unwashed, what would it be?" Reasonable question. Here are the topics I'd cover if I had five hours with the nontechnology senior management team, five hours to communicate what technology is all about, five hours to deliver a "program" of issues and opportunities, and five hours to get them thinking the "right" way about business technology.

First, it occurs to me that the program should be designed to be delivered as a whole or in parts, or in abbreviated form, with all of the parts compressed into a single presentation. Why all this fidgeting with the pieces? Because senior executives have ADD and there's no way to predict how long they'll sit still or how much time they'll actually commit to learning more about technology. Don't believe this? Test it by announcing a three-day program on "Business Technology for Nontechnology Executives" and see how quickly the screaming begins. Then see how many executives sign up.

Three modules make sense to me:

1. Technology architecture and infrastructure
2. Technology challenges and opportunities
3. Trends and best practices

The first module—*technology architecture and infrastructure*—should be designed to explain the basics: hardware, software, databases, communications and services. I suspect that many nontechnology executives don't understand "architecture" or "infrastructure." We need to make them feel comfortable about what they don't know, making sure that we don't embarrass anyone or make anyone feel uncomfortable about their knowledge of the basics. It should be treated as an "overview" of current technology, so the executives feel as though they are being updated rather than educated. (I'm sensitive to this aspect of bonding with executives: several times a year I present to the Wharton Advanced Development and CFO-as-Strategic-Partner Programs at the University of Pennsylvania, all very senior executives. The presentation to them is around "what they need to know" to optimize business technology management, not on lecturing them about what they don't know (although most of them know very little about technology, even the ones who run technology organizations at their companies.)

The second module—*technology challenges and opportunities*—should be designed to communicate the complexity of running technology architectures and infrastructures, and to communicate opportunities for business technology integration, especially the use of technology for cost management and competitive advantage. Examples here include network reliability, security, data synchronization, 24/7 eBusiness transaction processing, organization, and governance. The purpose of this module is to communicate the challenges that technology managers face as they deliver cost-effective technology services to a growing number of professionals. The module should also communicate opportunities for cost management and competitive advantage.

The third module—*trends and best practices*—should present some emerging technologies that could help the company save money and make money. This could be a fun module because it would demonstrate that there are technologies that can really help the company do some interesting and useful things. Some of the technologies to be covered would include business intelligence, web analytics, and selected Web 2.0 tools and techniques. You could show some short movies here. Executives like movies.

The overall objective of the program would be to bring executives and managers up to speed on technology environments, on technology challenges and opportunities, and technology trends and best practices.

The intended "effect" of the program should be:

- To deepen executive understanding of business technology and the important role it plays.
- To increase executive appreciation for the complexity of managing technology globally.
- To excite executives about technology as a significant lever for cost management and strategic advantage.

Form? Lots of case studies and war stories about the competition; that will really get them interested and keep them engaged. Can you spell "edutainment"?

TEN THINGS THE IT DEPARTMENT SHOULD TELL MANAGEMENT

The *Wall Street Journal* published an article in 2007, "Ten Things Your IT Department Won't Tell You," that lists some things you might do to get around your CIO's policies and procedures, things like how to download forbidden software or get your e-mail from lots of places when your corporate messaging server doesn't want to cooperate. I thought this was a stupid article. It was like I was reading about how 12-year-olds plot to confuse their parents to get more access to video games. After complaining to some friends about the whole premise of the article, one of them challenged me to turn the message around. "So, big shot, what would you tell 'management' about technology?" (Actually, they used a different phrase from "big shot.")

Here's what I'd say:

1. "First of all, 'management,' technology is an asset that needs to be nurtured—like a brand or a customer service reputation. If you don't invest in the asset, its value will fall, just as with any asset. Just ask Dell or Mercedes what happens when service and quality, respectively, suffer."

2. "And while we're talking about all this, remember that while operational technology has definitely commoditized, there are still strategic technology investments we need to be very careful about making. It's possible to make some major mistakes in the acquisition of all kinds of technology, so let's get some serious discipline in the technology acquisition process, and, please, don't listen too closely about killer apps at cocktail parties. Everyone knows that alcohol and technology don't mix."

3. "Don't forget that technology is still complex, even though industry standards have helped improve integration and interoperability. Listen, while there are fewer moving parts, the way we deploy them still makes the technology world tough to manage, and our vendors don't always help us."

4. "Please stop making exceptions to the governance process. If you want to save money and keep us agile, then do not allow all the flowers to bloom; instead, publish the standards and then stick with them. Every time you let someone off the hook, you make our life more complicated, and yours more expensive."

5. "Make the company's business strategy as transparent as possible (unless you really don't like talking about your own strategy or don't really have a strategy). The more the technocrats know about the business strategy, the more efficiently they will be acquire and deploy technology."

6. "Please make us account for our technology investments. Please make us link them to the business strategy and the impact each investment has on operational or strategic success. In spite of what you may think, we like ROI thinking. Hold us—and everyone—to it."

7. "Stop underestimating or overestimating the impact the web will have on business. I am really tired of our thinking that the web is just another channel. The web is not an evolutionary channel. It's definitely a revolutionary one that changes dramatically every year. Please allow us to pay close attention to new web technologies and web-based business models. By the way, why aren't we crowdsourcing our R&D? Make sure no one overhypes anything. Just because your idiot brother-in-law loves a technology doesn't make the technology lovable, or useful."

8. "Listen to my whining about the lack of a discretionary budget. I need some money to try new things. I need to fail fast and fail cheap but without a discretionary budget I can't do either."

9. "Please don't acquire any companies until I've looked at their technology. Never assume that our technologies will 'seamlessly integrate.' There's no such thing as seamless integration. Never assume that there are automatic technology gains that will result from a merger or acquisition. Nothing is farther from the truth."

10. "Invest in the right people with the right skills at the right price. Reward major contributors and prune out the losers. There's nothing else you can do to excite the troops more. They need to believe that productive work will be rewarded, and that lousy work will be punished."

What else would you like to say?

FINAL THOUGHTS ABOUT ORGANIZATION

This chapter makes a lot of arguments about governance, standardization, globalization and, of course, reorganization. There's also a fair amount of messaging involved in optimizing organizational structures and processes. But remember that structures and processes are ultimately organic: people make them work or fail. Structures and processes disconnected from their human enablers or failing to acknowledge personal financial reward structures will fail, and all of the people connected with them will become corporate failures who—no matter how hard they try—will never rebound from the stigma of doing the wrong thing at the wrong time for the wrong price.

We "organize" after we've figured out the competencies and motives of the team and how they might combine to make everyone some money. Organizations that organize before profiling their people, corporate cultures, or senior management team will inevitably fail because they're designing solutions that ignore the problems.

Structures and processes flow *from* people, cultures, and leaders, not *to* them. Make sure you understand this.

3

Management

This chapter examines at what we think we do as "managers." It also looks at some of the new management "best practices" that need to emerge for the business technology relationship to get to the next level.

The chapter begins, as do most of your days, with "Really Stupid Meetings." I don't even want to comment on how awful this actually is, because it will depress those of you predisposed to emotional outbursts and psychological traumas. Put a little differently, what kind of personal and professional life would you have if you didn't have to go to really stupid meetings? Could you get your work done? Could you avoid corporate idiots and sycophants? Could you actually manage your day? Stupid, wasteful meetings drain more productivity than sexually transmitted diseases, the federal deficit, and religion combined. We suffer through but get no relief from the endless parade of meetings, day after day, week after week, month after month, year after year, decade after decade. There is no escape. Sort of like the corporate off-sites that everyone loves. You know, the ones where everyone gets to bond with bongo drums, karaoke, and lounge lizard comedians hired to loosen everyone up after the group dinner which you are obligated to attend (and smile). Who comes up with this stuff? (This is why everyone hates HR.)

Management needs to manage to structures and processes that make sense to an organization, its people, leadership, and culture. Otherwise, you'll manage to abstract structures and processes. Management is about purpose. This chapter talks a lot about innovation. Can you think of a more important purpose? What about impact? Do total cost of ownership (TCO) and return on investment (ROI) still rule, or are they, as are so many other performance artifacts, corrupted metrics? Can you manage your way to the new technology delivery models, or are you stuck in the past because that's the way you've always done IT? What about risk management? There are new ways to think about risk that focus more on strategy than tactics. Leave traditional risk management to risk managers. Adult risk management is about lost and found strategic opportunities. Focus on a new risk equation. Finally, good management requires really tough business cases. I talk about what they look like at the end of this chapter along with some "final thoughts."

REALLY STUPID MEETINGS*

How do you vet ideas, kick off projects, discuss compensation, and reorganize? You go to meetings, and then you go to more meetings. And then you go to even more meetings. Are meetings the best way to solve problems? Absolutely not; in fact, meetings make things worse, make problems bigger, and empower idiots to stake influence claims on processes and outcomes.†

Do we need to talk endlessly about hardware and software upgrades? What about storage? How about open-source software? Should you upgrade your ERP suite after you've spent $300,000,000 deploying it? What are the issues here? Do you have the money, can you define the risk, and is the impact measurable? What else do you need to know?

After impact/cost/risk is assessed, meetings serve several purposes. First, they validate a decision that's already been made by smart people too polite to tell everyone that the decision has been made and no additional discussion is necessary, thank you very much. Meetings permit managers and executives to shout about how inclusive they are. They stretch out the decision-making process to acceptable process/outcome life cycles: everyone knows you cannot make big decisions fast, right? Meetings also provide a forum for deranged people, especially in political cultures that tolerate the participation of deranged professionals (because they'd rather put up with them than fire them).

---

* I wrote this while sitting in another really stupid meeting about technology issues that could be addressed in about 10 minutes. We've set aside three hours for this discussion. I am losing my mind.

† The guy speaking now is a complete moron who thinks he knows something about server farms; he ought to be on a pig farm.

Meetings have become the full-time job of meeting planners. There are actually people, lots of people, on the staffs of CIOs, CTOs, CEOs, CFOs, and COOs who do nothing but coordinate meetings. Internal meetings, external meetings, town hall meetings, leadership meetings, executive meetings, project meetings, strategy meetings, vendor meetings, metrics meetings, performance meetings, and even meta-meetings—meetings about meetings about meetings—like watching a television picture of a television picture in a television picture.

What should we do?* Let's keep meetings short; let's use our governance committees to publish a rule about the length of meetings. Let's say that no meeting can last more than 30 minutes and let's give door prizes to anyone who runs a shorter meeting (and pistol-whip everyone who runs longer ones). Let's remove the chairs from all of the conference rooms. People hate to stand around. The meeting I'm in now would have ended two hours ago if everyone were forced to stand. Brilliant. Never serve food or drink at a meeting. People hate to stand around without anything to eat or drink. Even more brilliant. Schedule meetings from 7 a.m. to 8 a.m. and 6 p.m. to 7 p.m. Get the governance cops to make this a rule. See how many meetings go away. Document meetings: publish the minutes of the meeting exposing how the time was spent and who said what. This is what a lot of churches do when they publish the names of their members and the amount of money they contributed to the church. When they do this, somehow, mysteriously, contributions increase. Maybe if we expose Harry for the idiot that he is, he might keep quiet or avoid meetings altogether. Get a digital damage meter that calculates the cost of each meeting as it's happening. Such a meter would display the cost of the meeting on flat panel displays all over the room by calculating the salaries of the participants and the time they're spending in the meeting. Just imagine what the cost of a stupid senior off-site would be?

What I need someone to do for me right now is call the meeting planner and inform them of an emergency I'm now facing, an emergency that will get me out of this really stupid meeting. Please save me.

---

* Can anyone get me out of this meeting? Another guy is now talking about viruses and all I can think about are the viruses I wish he had.

MANY HAPPY RETURNS

Let's keep ROI and TCO in perspective. You cannot build a business with these hammers. Are they important? Yes. Insightful? Usually. But obsessive-compulsive TCO/ROI behavior is as unhealthy as obsessive-compulsive quality, learning, or re-engineering behavior. Remember these?

The ultimate argument for a technology initiative is made in the business case. But key to good business cases is qualitative and quantitative data about the cost of a technology project's entire life cycle and the strategic impact it will have on meaningful business processes. TCO is about cost and ROI is about benefit.

Let's start with costs. There are acquisition costs, operational costs, and softer costs that are by nature more difficult to quantify. Total-cost-of-ownership calculations should also include costs over the entire life cycle of a hardware or software product. Softer costs include the cost of downtime, internal consulting that comes from indirect sources, and costs connected with your degree of standardization.

TCO data are an essential part of any business case which should ultimately be driven by the strategic or tactical return you expect to get from your investment. In other words, TCO data drive ROI data, which, like TCO data are both hard and soft.

Is it important to ask meaningful questions about why a business technology initiative exists and what impact it will have on the business (if it goes well)? Of course. So why is there so much disagreement about ROI? Research suggests that although many ROI methods are used, by far the most popular are ones that calculate cost reduction, customer satisfaction, productivity improvement, and contributions to profits and earnings. Two years is also considered by the majority of business technology executives as a reasonable time over which to measure ROI.

So what are the methods? One of the easiest is based on a simple calculation that starts with the amount of money you're spending on a business technology initiative (that includes TCO and other data) and then calculates the increased revenue or reduced costs that the investment actually generates. If a project costs a million bucks but saves two million then the ROI is healthy. Another simple method is based on payback data, the time it takes to offset the investment of the business technology initiative through increased revenues or reduced costs. If the payback period is short and the offsets are great then the project is "successful."

There are also methods based on economic value analysis or value added (EVA), internal rates of return (IRR), net present value (NPV), total economic impact (TEI), rapid economic justification (REJ), information economics (IE), and real options valuation (ROV), among too many others. Do we really need this much precision? (No.)

What about soft ROI? In the mid- to late-1990s, companies developed websites for a variety of reasons. First-generation sites were essentially brochureware, where very few transactions took place. What was the ROI on these sites? They did not reduce costs: in fact, they increased them. Nor did they generate revenue. They were built to convince customers, Wall Street analysts, investors, and even their own employees that they "got it," that they understood that the web was important. A significant intangible benefit? Absolutely.

Although I think that anyone who launches a business technology project without any TCO and ROI data is insane, I also appreciate the need for balance and reasonableness. This is why there's so much controversy about TCO/ROI. Lots of people think that too rigorous an application of TCO and ROI methodology will distort projects and perhaps even undermine business results. Others think that companies should know what to do instinctively and therefore shouldn't need a whole lot of data to make sound business decisions. Some think that the last thing they need to do is launch a training program to get their people up to speed on the latest and greatest approaches to TCO and ROI, that the time would be better spent just working the projects, and there are those who think that the effort to collect and analyze TCO and ROI data is disproportionate to the returns.

What to do? Simplicity, as usual, is your friend. Adopt a flexible approach to TCO and ROI. TCO data should feed ROI data which should feed the overall business cases for business technology decisions. Hard data are always better than soft data, but soft data, if they can be monetized (like generating a premium for your stock price or enhancing your brand), should also be analyzed.

The simplest approach to TCO data collection and assessment is a template that requires the collection of specific hard and soft data, and the simplest approach to ROI data collection and assessment is based on simple metrics that measure payback over a reasonable period of time. Payback should be defined around internal metrics such as cost reduction, and external ones such as improved customer service and profitability: not too complex, but meaningful. Some projects will pay themselves back in a year, whereas others may take three. Beyond three, things get too fuzzy, so I'd rethink projects with anything longer than three-year ROI tails.

TCO and ROI should not be used as clubs to bludgeon people: they should be used to inform decisions and monitor progress. (They should also play a role in the death of projects gone berserk.) In other words, TCO and ROI questions should always be asked, but the answers don't always need to be perfect.

A CRISIS IS A TERRIBLE THING TO WASTE

I have repeatedly argued that we have the opportunity to have IT both ways: to have IT save money and make money. I've also argued that we must deal with the crisis that the people who got us into the economic mess we're in today handed us (as they sip martinis purchased with bailout money). Yesterday someone said to me that a crisis is a terrible thing to waste, that there's always a silver lining, and if managed properly a crisis can be therapeutic, even productive. After saying goodbye to the last optimist on the continent, I started thinking about the implications of "good" crisis management (as Murphy whispered in my ear, "An optimist is someone who doesn't fully understand the situation").

Context defines options. When things are good, the "If it ain't broke don't fix it" crowd rules. "Management" is thankfully paralyzed when everyone's making money. Why start arguments that are unpleasant when you can play golf? Crises, on the other hand, force everyone to rethink almost everything, depending on the severity of the crisis. Today we have a major league crisis.

Technology spending will continue to fall after the dramatic decreases that began in 2009. Some CIOs I speak with tell me that 20% to 30% cuts are on the table. Thirty percent cuts are unrealistic without severely reducing services. (One CIO I know recently asked everyone to turn in their Blackberrys because the budget could no longer support Crackberry addicts, knowing full well that the outcry would be so loud that "management" would have to find some money to keep the addiction going.) But as unrealistic as the budget cuts might be, and as clever as some of us can be in the art of budget manipulation, there will be major cuts in people, hardware, software, and especially services. The crisis is bigger than any I have seen in decades, much worse than the dot-com crash of 2000. So where's the good news?

Let's try to see the crisis through an opportunity lens. What can we get done today that we could never hope to get done when things were good? How should we use the air cover of the current crisis to make the decisions that would have no chance of being made if things were OK? Think carefully about this because, we hope, the crisis will pass. There's a window of opportunity that will close after a suitable period of pain has passed.

First, look at the people. Do you have enough? Do you have too many? Do they have the right skills? And be brutally honest, because you only get to do this now: when things improve, the appetite for chewing up people will disappear. Do the high potentials still have potential or are they just high? Reorganization is the natural extension of people assessments (or is it the other way around?). Regardless of which comes first, crises provide opportunities to finally kill the ineffective PMO, promote the smart architects (and fire the dumb ones), and revamp the business relationship management office, among other organizational things you've been waiting to do.

Second, look at your processes. Now might be the time to redefine and reassert modern governance, especially in the technology intake area. Chances are good that you don't need any more projects, so shut down the demand for technology projects by defining acceptance criteria tightly. The governance around the procurement of hardware, software, and services should also be tightened. Take a look at business processes. Your business partners would kill for efficiencies that save and make money. Application development (if you're still doing it) can be redefined around agile and related methodologies. Think about mashups as a way to extend the functionality of your humongous enterprise applications.

Take a look at budgeting. One way to prioritize projects quickly is to draw a sharp distinction between discretionary and nondiscretionary projects. Nondiscretionary infrastructure projects can continue to be funded by the enterprise but discretionary projects should be funded completely by the business. This will help with technology demand and with project accountability. The last thing IT wants is a long list of underfunded projects destined to be late or likely to fail. Introduce chargeback accounting for all technology projects. This will provide accountability and transparency, both in short supply before the world came to an end.

Next, look at your partners and the contracts that tie you together. Now's the time to renegotiate *all* of them. Even if you're happy with a vendor's performance now's the time to insist on a better deal, which you can get because the vendor is way behind quota for last year and already for this year. You might also conduct a "stress test" of the relationship. Is the vendor a true partner or a pain in the ass? Does the vendor add measurable value or barely contribute to your business? Could you get along just fine with fewer vendors to which you give less money? Are the vendors that you've already hired fully utilized? It's time to revisit the SLAs (service-level agreements) that bind you together. It's time to introduce shared risk contracting and key-person clauses as well.

How about your hardware and applications? Assess your hardware architecture, server farms, data centers, and optimization technologies such as virtualization and voice-over-IP. Now is the time to "rationalize" the applications portfolio and think about whole new alternatives, such as open-source solutions and software-as-a-service. A lot of digital technology is redundant and expendable.

Make sure you exploit this crisis (and any others that come your way). We all know how reluctant companies are to do anything, let alone things that are controversial or confrontational. But when the building's on fire we'll do just about anything to get out alive. Now's your chance to fix some things you've been thinking about for years. Get to it before they put out the fire.

CHANGING OUR MINDS (ABOUT EVERYTHING)

We need to change our minds about everything. Quick: check on the ages of those in the cockpits of your companies. How many are over the age of 50? How many are older than 60? For every senior technology executive over the age of 60, add 100 points; for every one between the ages of 50 and 60 add 50 points. If you hit 1,000 points, you are absolutely positively doomed. If you hit 500 points you will die a slow death (until the senior executives themselves die, whichever comes first). If you're under 50 points, you can stop reading this chapter (but keep your eye on that 50-something executive who might be plotting a slow-down).*

Here's the deal. The world has changed, forever. First, hierarchical management structures will weaken as we continue to decentralize our business

---

* In the spirit of full disclosure, I am over 50 years of age, although not yet 60. But, you see, I no longer run a technology organization: I outsourced myself to consulting and teaching pastures where I can do relatively little damage. I'm also free from the inertia of the permanent rock formations that govern many large-enterprise technology organizations.

units globally. As I've argued throughout this book, we have to change the way we think about control, standardization, and the overall governance we bring to technology acquisition, deployment, and support. This will be hard because many of us fantasize our roles as technology Nazis screaming things like "No changes for you, one year!" Some of us have really enjoyed saying "No" to the business. This will end (or those of us who say "No" will "end"). Technology enables the business, not the other way around. If we haven't changed our minds about this fundamental maxim then we're in big trouble. Glass houses are morphing into clouds.

We need to change our minds about the safety we find in established vendors and their products. Yes, Microsoft, Oracle, and IBM make good stuff but so do Salesforce, Redhat, and JackBe. We don't need to buy everything veteran vendors sell just because they've been around forever and we know we can explain Microsoft, Oracle, and IBM to confused business executives and boards of directors. It's time to try some new providers, some new products, and some new acquisition models, even if they don't give us the best concert tickets.

Open-source is here to stay. Even the established vendors have "embraced" open standards. They have no choice. Do you? Yes, you can stay with proprietary software and pay the price or migrate to a hybrid software architecture that blends the best of both worlds. Who knows where all this will lead, but it's time to begin the migration toward openness and the freedom to express yourself. Symphony versus MS Office versus OpenOffice versus StarOffice? Siebel versus Salesforce.com versus SugarCRM. SQL Server versus MySQL. Yes.

Of course we'll all be renting hardware and software. Have you changed your mind yet about hardware- and software-as-a-service (HaaS/SaaS)? Have you spent any time in the clouds? Speaking at Oracle Openworld about cloud computing Larry Ellison said:

> The computer industry is the only industry that is more fashion-driven than women's fashion. Maybe I'm an idiot, but I have no idea what anyone is talking about. What is it? It's complete gibberish. It's insane. When is this idiocy going to stop? We'll make cloud computing announcements. I'm not going to fight this thing. But I don't understand what we would do differently in the light of cloud.

That's at least 50 points of wisdom. Cloud computing is not about how many servers or software applications you can rent, it's about shifting the locus of computing and communications technology outside the corporate firewall, redefining core competencies, and elevating vendor management to a real discipline. We need to change how we think about cloud computing from an incremental shift in technology offerings to a whole new way of acquiring, delivering, and supporting digital technology. I am glad that Larry does not plan to fight "this thing."

Will you let your people bring their computers to work? Or will they have to stay standardized on Dells, HPs, or Lenovos? Why? Try thinking about things differently. Maybe it's more about network connectivity than PC standardization. What about devices? Are you still deploying fat clients on some hardware migration or "refresh" schedule? Let's change our minds about all this. How many of us need fat clients with the amazing computing power they provide? Smart phones, which are really just mobile thin clients, are more than adequate for a huge segment of professionals in many companies. Why are we still living in the "break and fix" world of the 1980s and 1990s? Do you actually support PCs at your company? What if you changed your mind about thin versus fat clients, leasing versus buying, paying-by-the-drink versus paying-by-the-box, and matching computing and communications requirements to professionals who may or may not need anything more than a smart phone with a 3G browser? My guess is that we could all reduce our acquisition, deployment, and support costs by over 50% while providing more mobility and flexibility to our internal and external technology clients.

The whole concept of networks and networking is changing. We used to think about finite (and controllable) local and wide area networks (and then virtual private networks) as our communications highways, but all that's changed since the Internet emerged as a bona fide platform and interoperability and reuse emerged through service-oriented architectures. Networks are continuous, not discrete, as semiautomated and fully automated transaction-processing emerge as the raison d'etre of ubiquitous networks. By definition 100-pointers (aka old guys) will find it really hard to change their minds about open/continuous/ubiquitous network architectures because they scare the hell out of baby-boomers. Web 2.0 tools are redefining why we want communications and collaboration. Wikis, blogs, RSS filters, folksonomies, mashups, podcasts, social networks, crowdsourcing, and virtual worlds are pushing networks to new supporting roles, roles that are growing by leaps and bounds. Try putting the Web 2.0 genie back in the bottle. I dare you.

Let's all change our minds about people. Some of our people are ready, able, and willing to change with the times, but some are not at all interested in what tomorrow brings. You know what, and who, I mean. The exploitation of new technology is directly proportional to the trajectory of the changes we accept. Debating endlessly about whether open software, cloud computing, or SaaS has any merit is a waste of time, and most likely a diversionary tactic designed to slow if not outright kill, the pace of change.

Can we change our minds about everything? Maybe the first step is to get the points down to under 100. If anyone tells you that leadership doesn't matter, he's way over 50, and probably in charge. Leadership is key to perspective, strategy, and, yes, even vision: it's hard to see forward when age and experience have made you nearsighted. I have observed over the past few years that the massive changes in the field have fallen victim to all varieties of sabotage by 50- and 100-pointers. They've described the changes as risky, scary, stupid, not-ready-for-prime-time, expensive, insecure, and unlikely to scale, among other adjectives and accusations intended to keep SaaS, HaaS, open-source, cloud computing, and others at arm's length, at least until they pass away.

VITAMIN PILLS VERSUS PAINKILLERS

We're still in a recession. Our currency is still struggling. Inflation is worsening. Companies are worried. I addressed all this before. Now I'm extending the discussion about where to put technology dollars and how to pitch a recessionary budget.

Lots of technology gurus and pundits talk about the distinction between vitamin pills and painkillers. Put another way, there's an obvious distinction between investments that make money and those that save money, assuming, of course, that all goes well with the projects designed to save or make money. At the simplest level is the relationship between painkillers and cost management investments versus vitamin pills and investments designed to generate revenue.

So what will it be today and for the next year or two? (Yes, I think that this recession will be longer and deeper than the last few.) Painkillers, without a doubt. Those projects that contribute to cost reduction will be well received in many companies and those designed to generate revenue, vitamin pills, will be closely scrutinized. Continuing with some other metaphors, it may be better to buy or sell shovels as everyone looks for gold-plated growth. So is it time to buy shares in Cisco and EMC or Oracle and SAP? If you equate infrastructure with painkillers then Cisco and EMC make sense; if you see Oracle and SAP as vitamin pills then you may want to think twice about your investments in their products and services. Infrastructure projects are closer to painkillers and painkillers are closer to cost management than applications projects, vitamin pills, or revenue-generating projects.

The only problem with this is that it's all wrong. Although infrastructure projects often save money (and reduce pain), applications projects are where struggling companies should place their bets. Why? For the same reason that struggling companies in general should play offense rather than defense. This means that although cost management projects are always appealing, when times are tough companies should invest in projects that will eventually make them money. Throwing a pass on fourth and one is risky, but courageous and often very smart.

There's no question that projects must either save money or make money in a recessionary economy. But the relative distribution of these projects should be closely scrutinized. The conservative play is to invest only in projects that save you money, often in infrastructure projects that reduce some form of pain. But the smart play is to mix investments with as many, applications projects as possible, or more, that can contribute to revenue growth, so-called vitamin pills.

It's sort of like what contrarian stock market investors do. Does it work? More often than any of us cares to admit. So if you're about to present your technology budget, here's some advice:

1. Lead with painkillers likely to yield impressive cost savings; this will build credibility.
2. Selectively propose projects that look like they will save money and make money, knowing that they're more likely to make money than save it.
3. Manage the hell out of these projects: if they start to go south, kill them quickly and reload with another revenue-generating project (in cost-saving clothing).

Some of this requires some sleight of hand and some adult-sized hype. But if you want to emerge from this mess we're in as a hero, then work the system toward projects designed to score revenue gains, not just hold the competition to field goals.

SAVE MONEY, MAKE MONEY, OR GO HOME

We're in a prolonged recession (in spite of what the government "officially" tells us about the "official" definition of "recession"). Our currency is struggling. Inflation is back. Companies are worried. So what should we tell our bankers, the ones who control the technology budgets?

The KISS principle—keep it simple, stupid—always seems to apply, but in the current environment it's even more relevant. In a recent lunch with a senior (nontechnology) executive, he challenged me with a simple question: "What's in it for me?" "Simple," I said, "I can help you save money and make money with technology." As soon as I said it, I wished I had only offered one or the other, not both. So as the conversation evolved, I changed the message a bit to "I can help you save money *or* make money." Promising both outcomes might be suicidal.

Then we discussed technology trends. "What about hardware?" he asked. I told him that price/performance ratios are more favorable than ever and that new technologies such as virtualization, which I had to explain a little, can extend hardware (and software) capabilities pretty easily and cost effectively. Translation: hardware is cheaper; I can save money with hardware. But when we discussed the prospects for thin clients and the potential cost savings with their deployment, he went wild. Seems that he's always hated "fat clients," although he never called them fat, and always suspected that way too much money has been spent on the care and feeding of PCs. It's safe to say that at that point in the conversation I had his attention.

We discussed networking trends and how in the not too distant future corporate landlines may well disappear yielding to wireless communications of all kinds. "You mean I can kill all those landlines?" "Yes," I said. And what did he hear: less money.

The discussion about data was more about how to make money with technology. I explained that upselling and cross-selling were essentially data-driven business models that required some investments in things such as master data management, but that after these investments the potential for revenue generation was substantial. He liked that, and asked what his company was doing to make upselling and cross-selling possible.

When I told him that he might be able to replace Microsoft Office with an open-source alternative to liberate his company from whopping annual enterprise software licensing fees, he got even more excited. He demanded the list of open-source alternatives to the proprietary stuff he's been buying for decades.

I was leery of even bringing up SaaS but thought, what the hell, how many times do I get to talk to this guy about technology? I was worried that he might have a coronary when I explained how he could rent software (and hardware) instead of going down a multiyear implementation/deployment/support cycle. The idea that he could rent just about everything got him thinking about whether he should even be in the technology business. "So why am I spending hundreds of millions of dollars every year on technology?" he asked. I answered him with a question (why not?): "Is technology one of your core competencies, and, even if it is today, do you want it to be tomorrow?" This got him thinking. Maybe he should rethink his internal commitment to IT.

Rethinking is the key here. As things get tighter and expectations about the business value of IT increase, arguments for technology spending need to simplify around some core messages. "Save money or make money" is the argument, nothing more, nothing less. If you can shift the discussion to one or the other or (in a perfect world) both outcomes, you will get as much attention as you want. Then all you have to do is deliver.

TEN "NEW RULES" FOR IT

For those of you familiar with Bill Maher's "New Rules" on his HBO series *Real Time*, you might appreciate some new IT rules. (For those who don't know the show you might still appreciate the perspective represented by the following rules, which should be followed at all times.) Here we go:

1. CIOs should come from the business not the technology ranks: technology-rooted CIOs will never really understand the importance of business as *the* technology driver. When prospective CIOs start talking about network latency and virtualization it's time to get the hook out; go with the pro talking about upselling and cross-selling every time.

2. Business technology professionals should be grown in BT farms, the way we grow shrimp, salmon, and lobster. These pros, like the fish, will be tastier and freer of the toxins they may have picked up in data centers (which are known disease breeders).

3. Vendors are designed to be squeezed. Can anyone justify the margins that software or services vendors get? Please, if someone's going to get 50+% margins on their products and services they deserve to have someone hold them upside down and shake the cash out of their pockets.

4. Software is designed to be rented. Who, in 2011, in her right mind would embark on a five-year, five hundred million dollar implementation project? Only crack addicts would smoke this story. Even Microsoft, the mother of all enterprise software vendors, gets this.

5. Get over the lack of privacy. It's been gone for years and most Americans would sell their personal data for $50 a year, as long as you promised them a free Diet Coke. The fact is that privacy, like everything else in the world, is for sale at the right price.

6. Hardware, software, and services contract risk should be shared. Which professionals (besides lawyers) get to screw up and still get paid? The rule from now on is that performance should predict payment: no performance, no money.

7. Digital security is adequate. Yes, data will be stolen and transactions hacked, but by and large the web is secure enough to support all kinds of business-to-business and business-to-consumer transaction processing.

8. Colleges and universities need to revamp their business technology degree programs from the ground up, moving them at least to the late twentieth century. This would include rethinking degree programs in computer science, computer engineering, and management information systems, among other programs that deal with digital technology and how it supports business models and processes. The new rule is simple: if it's not relevant it doesn't go into the curriculum.

9. By 2012 the Wintel conspiracy will officially end and only thin clients will be permitted in 30 of the 50 states. The last 20 states must ban fat clients and bloatware no later than 2015.

10. Meritocracies will replace consensus-by-brothers-in-law-cronies-ex-girlfriends-ex-boyfriends-idiot-sons-and-daughters-and-golf-buddies, at least in this (if not a parallel) universe.

GUERILLA BUDGETING

There's never enough money. I'm tired of hearing this complaint. Of course there's never enough money. Everyone wants more money, which is why there's never enough. United States companies are better at cutting costs than they are at growing their businesses, so there's less money in our companies to do anything meaningful. The government has already spent itself into oblivion, screwing our kids and grandkids in the process, so there's no money there for essential things such as health care and education (although there always seems to be enough money to wage war). Many of us have huge mortgages so we don't have enough money for even modest vacations or college tuition for the same screwed kids.

Technology budgets are always under attack. Most of these budgets have little or no discretionary room to maneuver. So when the boss says "What about that Web 2.0 stuff? What are we doing there?," most CIOs and CTOs tell them, "We're looking at it," knowing full well that they only have enough money to put out the daily brush fires and nothing more. Exacerbating the shortage of cash, operational technology (infrastructure, PCs, laptops, PDAs, cell phones, messaging, and the like) is expected to cost less every year. After all, everything's a commodity, isn't it? And everyone knows how flat the world is.

Let's talk about guerilla budgeting. First, if I'm a CIO or CTO, I'm not telling anyone how my investments distribute across my operational versus strategic priorities because I can't draw a clean line myself, and because I want to make sure that I don't create a budgeting target which the CFO might lock onto, like a laser weapon. In fact, I need to protect whatever discretionary latitude I have because I need to be strategically, not just operationally, responsive to the company's requirements. Because I can't (and really don't want to) draw clean lines between all of my strategic and operational projects, I will push all of the gray area projects into the strategic category. This will insulate them from the cold of commoditization and the expectation that "this should be cheaper."

I will also campaign for new strategic projects with the senior management teams of the enterprise and the lines of business (especially the ones that juice their compensation packages). This is marketing, pure and simple. I need to convince them that I can help them solve some of their most pressing problems including, of course, cost management, but also customer service, cross-selling, up-selling, and anything that leads to profitable growth and larger personal bonuses. If I'm a really good sales-person I can convince them to pay for the new initiatives as add-ons to my budget. These should be sold as special projects with pilot phases that pro-vide enough information to determine if a major initiative makes sense. These are classic win/win's inasmuch as I get more money to invest in strategic projects and the business feels good about using technology to solve major business problems.

I'm also going to squeeze my vendors so tightly that they cough up cash all over the floor if they want to keep my business or want new business from me. The strategic pilots that I do for the lines of business should be at least partially subsidized by vendors with vested interests in the outcomes. A rule of thumb is 10% of the eventual project cost, where a $10,000,000 project would have a subsidy value of $1,000,000. After they stop crying, they will accept the terms. (Of course, the quid pro quo is that if the project escalates to full value, the subsidizing vendor will get the deal.)

I am going to create some major incentives for my people. I will develop some payback metrics that require ideas to have at least a 3X return. If one of my team can save me a ton of money in the delivery of operational technology, for example, then I will pay him a bonus equal to one third of the savings. The reverse equation would apply to generating revenue. This will require internal service-level agreements with my own people, but it could be well worth the effort. I would only pay them when the savings or revenues are realized. Try this and watch what happens. Forget crazy glue: money is the most powerful glue on the planet.

I am also going to think about my own top line. How can I make money with technology? What can I sell? If I have excess computing and com-munications capacity, I might try to become a reseller. There is precedent for this. Companies have been providing services to other companies for years. Even expertise is resold, especially in the area of architecture. In a previous life, I bundled architectural and database management expertise into consulting offerings that I sold to noncompetitors. My internal people always had lots to do; however, they were able to find a few days a month to consult for a share of the fees. They also learned a lot by working outside the proverbial box. These steps might help you with technology budgeting. Think about them and then try them out.

ANOTHER AUDIT?

One of the steps that more and more companies are taking is the conduct of "optimization audits." Just what we need: another audit, another acronym (OA), and another question to answer when someone higher in the organization than you asks about how optimization audits work and if they're required by some government agency.

They're not required; they're not part of anyone's formal compliance agenda. But they do make a whole lot of sense. Several companies I work with have requested them because they've made some major technology investments and they'd like to know if they're getting the bang for the buck they expected (and were told to expect by the vendors who provided the hardware and software and consultants who assisted in the implementation of the monster applications or rejuvenated infrastructure).

Optimization audits look at existing computing and communications infrastructures and applications, and assess their potential value to sales, marketing, growth, and profitability. These audits are different from the more conventional TCO or ROI assessments that companies often make before they approve business cases for new technology projects. Optimization audits focus on unexploited business value from investments already made. Put another way, they're designed to answer the question, "What the hell did we get for the $100,000,000 we just spent? And you better not tell me that all we got for all that cash was a zero latency network."

The greatest need for OAs is in companies that have made major investments in enterprise resource planning (ERP), customer relationship management (CRM), business intelligence (BI), and network and systems management (NSM) applications. The price tag for these investments can easily exceed $100,000,000. But there's a life-cycle problem with these mega applications: implementations tend to consume so much time, money, and effort that payback tends to be tactical and operational for way too long, and to the relative neglect of strategic payback. For example, let's assume that a company implements an ERP system to integrate disparate financial reporting systems. Most of the effort is devoted to the consolidation of financial data and the standardization of financial reporting. Although operational efficiency is obviously valuable, the existence of a common transaction-processing platform enables much more than standardized reporting of financial data. An ERP application, for example, can integrate back-office, front-office, and virtual-office (Internet) applications. If the databases are also standardized across these applications then cross-selling and up-selling may be possible, along with supply chain integration and even dynamic pricing. CRM applications can help define "whole customer" models with long-term life cycles that can be monetized year after year. These are the kinds of dividends that enterprise applications can yield if they're pushed to their full capacity, capacities that even the vendors themselves often fail to stress. In their desire to sell operational solutions they sometimes fail to sell the longer-term strategic impact of their technology.

Optimization audits are designed to answer the following kinds of questions:

- Now that we have a standardized (ERP, CRM, BI, NSM) platform, what are the quantitative tactical and operational returns on the investment we're seeing?
- What are the potential tactical and operational benefits we're *not* seeing?
- What strategic benefits are we seeing?
- What strategic benefits are we *not* seeing?
- How can the business be transformed by the efficiency of the platform and its possible extensions?

Optimization audits take a top-down approach to model holistically the company's information, product, and service processes, and their relationship to the standardized platform they've implemented. The top-down profile is informed by the existence of the enterprise platform (which, more often than not, is implemented from a set of bottom-up priorities). The last step is the connection to business value metrics, such as sales, growth, and profitability.

Optimization audits should be conducted by companies that have implemented large enterprise applications or massive infrastructure platforms for primarily tactical or operational reasons. Although these reasons are solid, they're incomplete. Additional strategic payoff should be defined, and pursued, as vigorously as tactical and operational payoffs were pursued. But remember that strategic payoff is only meaningful when it's defined around business, not technology, metrics. The days are long gone when a CIO can authorize a $100,000,000 project to make some applications talk to one another or manage technology assets more cost effectively. It's no longer about just cost management: it's now and forever about growth and profitability. Optimization audits are all about finding the optimal path from technology to profitable growth.

INNOVATION IN FLIGHT

On more than one occasion in my career someone has used the metaphor about changing an engine in flight. Yes, it's hard to fix things in motion, or to be creative when budgets are tight. But when times are tough we need to (cheaply and quickly) innovate more than when things are good. But how?

The industry pundits report that technology spending fell by about 5% in 2009. (I'm not sure where they get their numbers: the CIOs I work with are struggling with cuts ranging from 10% to 25%.) CAPEX projects are being killed as fast as global warming is being debunked by Republicans. Projects with payback periods less than 12 months are not even on the radar screen. If the project doesn't save money or make lots of it, it's not a project. It doesn't even exist. In spite of what the pundits are telling us— that this too shall pass—we are in a bona fide nuclear winter. Imagine pitching a new innovative project that will transform the business, or a project that completely redefines how you relate to your customers, or a project that will once and for all kill all of the competition. Do you think these projects would fly? I cannot imagine the discussion that a five-year $300,000,000 ERP project proposal would trigger.

Innovation should be fast, cheap, and effective. Risk should be manageable. The new business case for an innovative project is exactly the same business case that should exist when economic times are good, although good times permit longer-term perspectives, longer payback windows, and bigger appetites for risk. Let's look at how to motivate the troops to the nirvana of fast/cheap/effective/not very risky innovation.

INNOVATION PARAMETERS

Innovation, like all business activities, occurs in a context, a situation that defines the parameters of what's possible and what's acceptable. Even companies whose core competency is innovation are throttling back their innovation activities. Of course, this makes no sense, but what does? Investing in AAA-rated CDOs from Citigroup made no sense, just as paying failed human beings millions of dollars for the destruction of their companies makes no sense. Ceasing innovation makes no sense. So what works in the current climate? Here's a five-pronged approach to innovating in flight.

Incentives

Step one is to revisit and redefine incentives. The suggestion is not to increase everyone's salaries (and bonuses); we've done that enough, but to tap into everyone's desire to demonstrate just how creative they are and everyone's desire to make more (and more) money. This is the perfect time to create a generous "pay-you-later" innovation initiative. The concept taps into two human motivations: the desire for cash and the desire to be respected.

Pay-you-later (PYL)-based innovation creates very real, but postponed, incentives to innovators. Similar to a stock option that vests over time, PYL financial incentives create "shares" whose value is tied directly to the future payback of the innovation effort. This requires that we develop credible performance metrics that measure the impact the innovation effort actually has. For example, if an employee develops an alternative manufacturing process that yields cost savings, he or she should receive a financial reward. If an employee figures out how to turn angry customers into loyal ones, then he or she should be rewarded, as long as the turns can be measured.

The key to innovation in tough times is the creation of incentives designed to unleash creative thinking. But the incentives must be PYL-based, because the budget cannot withstand front-loaded rewards for innovation projects that may or may not succeed. The key is to incentivize employees to work longer and harder than they already do, for the promise of reward.

Incentives that drive the most aggressive behavior are financial, but there are other incentives as well, including flexible work schedules, support to stay current in a field, funds to travel to selected professional conferences, and other expressions of recognition and achievement. But make no mistake about it: extra cash is the most powerful incentive yet to be invented, especially these days. If it can be demonstrated that creative employees can make a lot of money innovating at their companies, there will be innovation. This approach opens the innovation process to as many professionals as choose to play. This is a departure from innovation models that segment innovators from the rest of the team and funding them from designated innovation budgets. Tweaking incentives around and beyond traditional innovation rewards is a sign of the times.

Governance

There should be rules about what counts and what doesn't. Many of our governance policies fail because of their ambiguity. Specificity is critical in crises. The worst thing we can do is leave innovation processes and rewards to the interpretation of corporate bureaucrats who inevitably confuse even the most diligent innovators.

The location and control of innovation should be part of the governance policy, as should the innovation funding policy (see below). The nature of innovation activities and the measurement of their impact should be specified. Business case templates should be developed by the company to assure the vetting of ideas. Specific due diligence criteria should be identified and defined for the innovators to use. A due diligence process should also be defined. Put another way, if an employee wants to innovate, then she should be provided with a kit full of criteria and processes that together define an innovator's business case for a specific project.

Clearly there are innovation processes already in place at most, if not all, companies. Some companies have large research and development (R&D) budgets. There may even be some tacit incentive programs around innovation "suggestions." The suggestions here call for special governance around innovation by anyone who wants to innovate. As internal R&D budgets get slashed, we need to broaden the innovation mission across the entire company. We also need to define an innovation process that our suppliers, partners, and even customers can implement. How might this work? Incentives can be created for nonemployees to innovate around the relationships they have with companies. Regardless of the specific governance a company defines around innovation it should be specific, disciplined, and decentralized.

Funding

In tough economic times, it's essential that innovation funding be located where the impact of the innovation effort will be felt. The idea of innovation as a shared service is wrong-headed; the idea of innovation as discretionary initiatives by those closest to the impact the initiatives will have makes sense. Funding is directly traceable to the beneficiary, who assumes all of the innovation risk (which should be eminently manageable). This is a departure from large centralized research and development organizations that prosper during good times but get cut during bad times. Funding can come directly from the line of business interested in innovating to save money or make money. The key in this climate is to unleash funding from nontraditional sources of innovation and (as suggested above) adjust the governance around who owns innovation.

Initiatives

Remember that innovation initiatives must be fast, cheap, and effective (with minimal risk) or they shouldn't be discussed. What kinds of initiatives look like this? There are several that should be considered.

The first is *crowdsourcing*. Crowdsourcing is an innovation process that can be implemented to expand your network of really smart people for very little money. Among others, www.InnoCentive.com and www.NineSigma.com are sites that broker R&D problems between companies and independent smart people (ISPs) for very little money (relative to maintaining and rewarding internal smart people [SPs]). Crowdsourcing can be extended to lots of innovation activities. Internal crowdsourcing can be implemented in conjunction with external crowdsourcing. It's fast and cheap and can extend expertise as far as the web can see.

Another approach to innovation is through *acquisition*. There's no better time to buy companies, and their intellectual property (IP), than today. Valuations are extraordinarily low. It's now possible to acquire all kinds of IP for a song (and a little cash and stock). It's time to copy CISCO, which for years has acquired as much IP as it has created. The acquisitive innovation model is more than viable today when companies, technologies, and IP are all cheap.

Yet another approach is through *joint ventures* (JVs) and *other strategic alliances*. Companies need each other now more than ever. One company's core competency is another's skills gap. There are opportunities for companies to partner in numerous ways. Spinning out companies in joint ventures with shared equity ownership can make a lot of sense. When structured properly, JVs can generate a lot of innovation in a shared services model that can serve all parties well. Agreements to innovate jointly with partners can save time and money. Of course, not all corporate cultures will be willing to partner with companies that might become their competitors or, because of the arrangement, only earn a share of the jointly generated IP. Some managers and executives would never share anything; others would never even consider posting a problem on www.InnoCentive.com or www.NineSigma.com. There's not much anyone can do about Luddites.

Finally, there's a slate of internal initiatives that can be pursued. These initiatives are the ones that speak directly to low cost, low risk, and high impact, and work within the parameters of the current economic situation. In addition to the above opportunities, companies should encourage, incentivize, and manage a slate of initiatives likely to yield meaningful innovation.

Assessment

It's important to assess the impact of all innovation steroids. Early termination, or stimulation, is the way to go. The proactive assessment of innovation projects breaks with tradition: how many failed technology initiatives continue to get funding? Unfortunately, most companies are far from perfect killers. Way too many projects exist beyond all hope of success. Tough economic times call for draconian ongoing assessments. Performance metrics should be specific, quantitative, and continuously measured. The air cover of the economic crisis can perhaps improve the discipline around killing or accelerating specific initiatives. Again, a crisis is a terrible thing to waste.

Innovation is challenging in good times. But in tough times, we need to reduce (or even eliminate) the major obstacles to success. Tweaking incentives, governance, and funding enables the launching of initiatives that can yield huge dividends. Tweaking obstacles includes tweaking corporate cultures, the quality of corporate leadership, and the extent to which "politics" permeates the culture, among other mitigating factors. This means that although we know how to innovate in flight we still struggle with execution.

WHY STRATEGIC RISK MANAGEMENT IS SO IMPORTANT

The classic business case focuses on projects, portfolios, and strategies. Each of these initiatives is assessed with reference to value, cost, and risk. Or you can use SWOT (strengths, weaknesses, opportunities, and threats) analysis if you like. The traditional juxtaposition is between initiatives and their likely payoff in the context of what might go wrong and what the initiatives might cost. There are all sorts of elaborate methods, tools, and techniques used to vet alternative initiatives. Companies specialize in providing consulting support to companies seeking to rank-order initiatives, develop business cases, organize pilot demonstrations, and otherwise help them make the right decisions at the right time for the right price. I'm always amazed at how corporate knitting gets outsourced so often: shouldn't everyone be able to develop a business case?

Within the business case, we tend to think about risk in negative terms. We define risk along a series of continua that project high/medium/low risk onto aspects of a project as well as the overall project itself. There are people risks, technology risks, scheduling risks, and risks to the organization if the project fails, having consumed some precious resources that cannot be redirected toward another (less risky) project. We also talk a lot about risk mitigation. Most companies that have institutionalized the business case development process or have formal project management offices, require project managers to develop a risk mitigation plan.

Risk is what chief financial officers (CFOs) usually emphasize. "What can go wrong?" "What will it cost us if the wheels come off this project?" "What happens if the vendor goes belly up?" "What do we do if the chief architect has a heart attack?" These are the kinds of questions that CFOs love to agonize over. They also love to beat the business case team over the head with these and any other risk-related question they can imagine.

Risk assessment and mitigation are core to a business case that assumes something will be done and that there's a possibility that something will go wrong. Murphy of "Murphy's Law" fame is a riskophile. He loves everything there is to love about risk. Ultimately, he warns us that most projects should just be shelved because they bring too much risk to the table.

Projects, programs, portfolios, and other corporate initiatives are about identifying and managing risk. But what about the risks connected with avoiding initiatives? What if all of the initiatives an organization avoids are strategic?

STRATEGIC RISK MANAGEMENT

There are any number of initiatives that companies forgo for a variety of reasons. Most companies are risk averse. But what about the initiatives that fall through the cracks of the vetting and due diligence processes, the initiatives that never even result in a business case? It may well be that what companies do not do creates the greatest risk. In other words, what about the risk of strategies that minimize risk by making the funding criteria so stringent that hardly any projects make it through the vetting process? What is the risk of a bad strategy? What is the risk of avoiding alternative technology delivery models? What's the risk of yielding to the inertia of "how we do things?" Risk Nazis love to derail specific operational projects. What might they say about flawed business technology strategies?

THE NEW RISK EQUATION

Strategic risk should be forward thinking, proactive, and opportunity-driven. In fact, the cost of not doing something should be measured creatively and—as counterintuitive as it may seem—quantitatively.

So what are the strategic opportunities that are simultaneously risks? First and foremost, it's the management of the overall business technology relationship. The debate about "alignment" has persisted for decades (and fueled thousands of stupid debates), but the realities of the agile organization have passed the debate by, by a country mile. No one needs to argue about the importance of IT any longer. No one needs to think about reporting relationships that will encourage communication among business and technology professionals. We're way past all that. The question now focuses on how wide and deep the relationship should be, and the consequences of defining the relationship poorly.

Business technology relationship management (BTRM) is an opportunity and a risk. When done right it can increase the payoff of technology investments. When done poorly or not at all, it can cost a company money, time, and employee productivity. The risk impact of avoiding BTRM is very high.

The next strategic risk is sourcing. Only someone who's lived on another planet for the past few years is unaware of the impact of alternative technology delivery models. Core competency assessments are something we've all done from time to time; however, the need for them now is at an all-time high. Competition can be found down the road or across the globe. If a company is making or servicing the wrong things, with the wrong processes and cost structures, it will die from the blow of a competitor who might just as well be invisible as in its face. Such is the result of the eBusiness bandwagon we all so eagerly jumped on in the late 1990s. Understanding what business works and what doesn't is paramount to twenty-first-century companies. Is the acquisition, deployment, and support of technology part of the expertise a company wants or needs to have? Should companies continue to home-grow and customize technology? Or has it become fully commoditized? The strategic risk of getting sourcing wrong is huge.

What about business process modeling and new business models? Not establishing a center of excellence in BPM (business process management) is risky. How can a business remain competitive and efficient without understanding and mapping, at a detailed level, the processes that together define its business model? How can a company invest in manual BPM when there are countless software tools that enable even the most complicated modeling? (Yes, there are still many companies who keep their business processes modeled on paper and, maybe, in a spreadsheet.) The risk of not doing BPM is similar to the risk of never going to the doctor or getting a blood test. You don't know what you don't know, which makes many managers happier than knowing about problems they have to fix (or processes they have to improve).

Investments in new technology present opportunities and risks. What is the risk of avoiding advanced technologies? Or coming so late to the party that the lights are already off? Three cases in point: virtualization, voice-over-IP (VOIP), and software-as-a-service. Virtualization saves money, sometimes lots of money. VOIP is also cost effective. SaaS relieves all kinds of pressure from already strapped internal technology staffs. A few years ago all of these technologies, although doing fine, were not what most analysts would have called "mainstream." But two years ago they were, and today they're tried, true, and fully exploitable. Jumping in now makes sense, whereas jumping in a couple of years ago made much better sense. We're not talking about early adoption of bleeding-edge technologies here. We're talking about the monitoring of technologies likely to pay large dividends to those who adopt them at the right time and place in their evolution. The ability to do this is a strategic capability. Existing without this capability is risky and expensive.

What about investments in people? How many corporate strategies talk about the importance of "talent management?" How many actually mean it? Words are easy and cheap. Investments are the indicators of strategic value. At the end of the day, without the right people all organizations suffer. What's the risk of losing your best people? What's the risk of having your best people recruited away? What's the risk of keeping your people well-steeped in old technology?

These five strategic opportunities/risks define success. One simple drill: ask why these five strategic initiatives have not been pursued in your organization. Assess the response. Is the answer, "We don't have enough money to fund things like this"? Is it, "These kinds of things only generate soft ROI"? Or, is it, "We've tried these kinds of things in the past and they didn't work out"? These are the answers of managers and executives who are willing to accept the risks associated with the failure to make the right strategic decisions. The trick is to develop a list short enough to attract the no-brainer crowd. Put another way, it's always effective to argue with "When did you stop beating your wife" logic: who can oppose strategic decisions that reduce risk? Try finding someone willing to say that she doesn't believe in investing in her people, or that all new technologies are all hype, or that insight into the company's business processes is unnecessary. Ask what the feeling is about improving the relationship between the business and technology professionals at the company. Or how everyone feels about optimizing the company's relationships with its vendors.

Strategic risk discussions are especially important today because of the nature, location, and speed of competitors. The days of "owning" a market are long gone. Companies struggle on a daily basis to survive, let alone grow profitably. The irony is that when times are tough we focus on the operational and tactical, squeezing as much money from these areas as we can. But the real money lies in strategic initiatives with longer tails. It's a pity that so many managers see crises only as green lights to cut costs (and people and processes) rather than launch the right long-term strategic initiatives. Is your company tactically tight but strategically weak? Maybe it's time to reassign the risk Nazis to more important duty.

INNOVATION ON THE CHEAP; MOVING FORWARD WHILE STANDING STILL

It's no secret that these are tough times. Technology budgets are being slashed over and over again. CFOs are running wild, attacking every budget that cannot be justified logically, financially, and politically. If the ROI is not bulletproof, it's not real. CEOs are by and large in bunkers protecting their turf (not to mention their salaries, bonuses, stock options, and "separation packages," the golden parachutes that have everyone as angry as they can be, though not quite as angry as the commandeering of corporate jets for family getaways to Paris, Cabo, and Dubai).

But the need to develop new products, solve tough R&D problems, creatively improve customer service, and re-engineer business processes has never been greater. The tension between spending money to innovate and improve, and the absolute requirement to cut costs to survive and remain competitive is electric. Unfortunately, the need to cut costs to survive and remain competitive is winning: survival always trumps growth. Budgets for "innovation" generally or for specific innovation projects are all but gone in many companies. Innovation initiatives are placed unceremoniously in "nice to have" bins where in tough times "discretionary" projects go to die.

As suggested earlier in this chapter, the priority clearly has got to be on innovation projects that are fast and cheap and likely to have huge payoffs. Put another way, innovation initiatives must be low risk, low cost, and high value. Anything else? Yes, they need to be defensible in a climate increasingly neurotic about business cases and project approvals. They must have clear relative value and minor opportunity costs. They also cannot be sold as "transitional," overly "strategic," or as "must have" projects. If they're sold that way they will attract way too much attention at a time when flying under the radar screen is the only way to fly. The last thing anyone wants to do is create high-profile projects that require constant care and feeding and incessant internal marketing. If I were selling fast/cheap/effective innovation projects in this climate, I'd soft pedal the work, making sure that I managed expectations down to uncontroversial levels. I'd bootstrap funding as best I could. I'd also enlist some courageous business partners to provide air cover for new projects that will inevitably attract attention, even if they are conceived as low-key, low-cost initiatives. Sound defensive? It is. When there's no money one must get as creative as possible and proceed very, very carefully. So let's look at ways to accelerate innovation-on-the-cheap.

WAY OVERDUE—YET STILL REALLY CHEAP: BPM

The way to market business process management projects is to embed them in "what we do every day, anyway" descriptions. Many large enterprises already own BPM software applications; even smaller ones have them or have access to them. The key is to map the processes that drive your company and catalogue them according to their relative efficiencies and contributions to cost management or profitable growth. Once that step's completed, you can modify them in a simulated software environment to determine how improvements would affect key performance metrics. The problem with BPM initiatives is that they are time consuming and expensive, and this is not the time to launch time-consuming or expensive initiatives of any kind. But innovation is dependent upon, among other things, process re-engineering.

So how can we get the best thinking about process innovation without paying an arm and a leg? There are several ways. First, empower your customers, suppliers, and partners to improve your processes. This group has enormous insight into what you do well and poorly and it's in their vested financial interest to help you re-engineer the processes that affect how you interact with them.

The second suggestion is to empower business owners to re-engineer their processes for a "fee." Part of the general suggestion here is to use positive incentives to spur innovation (see below). BPM can be incentivized as easily as any activity we're trying to encourage or, in this case, re-engineer. Who better than the owners of business processes to suggest how they should be improved? Once they achieve results, reward them.

A third idea is to enlist one or more BPM software vendors to conduct "subsidized" pilots on your behalf. The deal here is pretty simple: in exchange for the re-engineering of your processes you will, if the results are effective, assist the vendor in the development of white papers, interviews, and reference accounts. Ultimately, you may hire the vendor to assist in additional re-engineering efforts. Finally, there are graduate schools everywhere. Why not offer process re-engineering as class projects and masters and doctoral theses for eager, and smart, graduate students? Believe me when I tell you how excited they would be to work on real problems for real companies. BPM can be inexpensive.

CROWDSOURCING FOR FUN AND PROFIT

Expand your team without expanding the team. There are lots of very smart people living on the web who can be enlisted to help solve many of your tough R&D problems. I have argued several times here that R&D crowdsourcing is a cost-effective way to pursue a variety of innovation projects. Innocentive and NineSigma (www.innocentive.com and www.ninesigma.com, among other platforms) expand your R&D staff without hiring anyone. In fact, R&D crowdsourcing represents an alternative innovation delivery model that should be piloted by far more companies than post problems on the major sites today. Is crowdsourcing R&D outsourcing? Yes, but the model is more discrete than continuous: specific problems are posted as targets for freelancers to attack, for a fee. Problems come and go and have life cycles. Companies incentivize independent thinkers to develop creative solutions as quickly as possible. In tough economic times, why wouldn't everyone in the R&D business post some problems and see what happens?

There are other crowdsourcing possibilities. Why not think about help desks and support for specific applications? What about challenging the crowd to develop new processes in your vertical industry? What about new product development? There are a number of ways to engage the crowd. You can use hosting services (such as the ones mentioned above) or you can blog/post the problems yourself. Crowdsourcing represents an incredibly cost-effective way to innovate. In fact, it can become part of a company's overall sourcing strategy. Why buy smart people when you can rent them?

TELL THEM YOU LOVE THEM—TO INNOVATE

There's a lot of creativity in your workforce. But they're probably not empowered to think and act creatively. As always, it's all about incentives and incentives management. I do not understand why companies do not exploit incentives to achieve all sorts of operational and strategic results. Regardless of the economic times or the financial state of the company, incentives management is a strategy that everyone should pursue.

In tough times, when no one expects much of a raise or a bonus, the corporate reward structure must be reassessed. Reassessment will provide a path to offset some of the anger and alienation that occurs when the corporate bank is closed. Funny how employees expect to be rewarded for their work, and how they get angry when they're not. Reassessment can also provide insight into how to motivate disenfranchised employees during a stingy time.

As discussed above, a set of specific incentives should be developed that focus directly on innovation. Innovation performance metrics should be defined. A reward matrix should be published so everyone can see how innovation will be rewarded. The idea is to re-engage employees in a win/win process. The idea is to get them thinking and working: for a price.

The performance metrics must be specific and quantitative. For example, ideas that shorten the new product design life cycle should be rewarded based on some calculation of what it costs to move products through life cycles. Similarly, the ability to exploit intellectual property for new product development should be rewarded based on the time it takes to locate and secure IP used to develop new products and services. New processes, especially if the current ones have been catalogued, can be rewarded based on cost savings or revenue generation, or combinations of these metrics.

SOCIAL MEDIA (POOR MAN'S MARKETING, CUSTOMER SERVICE) AND INNOVATION

We don't need to go to Peoria anymore. We can test products and services in lots of interesting and cheap ways: blogs, wikis, RSS filters, and even virtual worlds can be used to test new products and document the reactions that customers have to the products. Social media tools are inexpensive and ubiquitous. Social networking can be used proactively and reactively. Proactively, it can be used to plant and nurture ideas. Reactively, all social media can be used to assess opinions about new products, services, and whole brands.

The social media listening area is growing quickly because customers are spending more and more time in blogs, wikis, social networks, and virtual worlds. What are they talking about in these media? It's extremely cheap to listen to social media directly or with the help of vendors with the ability to listen and profile products, services, companies, and brands. Radian6, BuzzMetrics, Umbria, and ListenLogic are the leaders in this space. ListenLogic is especially smart (with some proprietary semantic processing) and is more of a social media business intelligence platform than a social media listener. These companies can assist you in new product design, development, deployment, and assessment.

It's amazing how reluctant companies are to exploit inexpensive solutions to old problems. Open-source software, virtualization, and social media are just a few of the solutions the industry has given us to save money (and make money). Innovation is served by all of them. Social media are an especially powerful innovation technology.

INNOVATION TALENT DEVELOPMENT THAT YOU ACTUALLY MEAN

Every company on the planet talks a good game about the importance of talent development. Hardly any of them really mean it. It's an obligatory pillar of every corporate strategy: talent development, "Because we understand how important our people are to us." Who believes this? Only some of the employees: senior management doesn't usually believe it. The competition usually doesn't believe it. Certainly the families of the employees usually don't believe it. In fact, they never believe it.

When taken really seriously, talent development is what the military calls a "force-multiplier." Smart motivated professionals pay huge dividends (as long, of course, as they are well incentivized). But the commitment to their development must be well conceived and long term, and probably not best left to the HR professionals. Instead, talent development should occur in the functional areas where their talent will be applied. But how should your people be developed in an age of scarcity? The first step is to ask the professional to develop his or her own professional development program. This program will provide you with the employee's perspective on what he needs to be successful for you, and for himself. It will also provide you with evidence that you, as a manager or executive, actually care about the employee: the wonderful Hawthorne effect occurs every time you express interest in one of your employees. You should then engage a professional talent scout to assess each of your employees and her programs with reference to your requirements. The results of this process will identify the keepers (and all of the others) and the list of things they should be doing, once they receive the right education and training. If you really believe in talent development this is the smallest investment you should make.

Expertise is not genetic. It can be acquired. If there's a commitment to talent development it should include a commitment to innovation expertise. Learning to innovate is a talent that should be developed and nurtured. Mentoring, classes, internships, and whatever else works should be encouraged to improve the processes by which your employees innovate.

Will all this be expensive? Only the back end with the talent scouts, but there are really good talent scouts out there who don't cost much money. The process described above should be formalized in a center of excellence or at least a codified business process standardized as a key corporate process. Although all this requires some investment, the dividends are potentially huge. But a word of caution: if a long-term commitment to talent development isn't there then you shouldn't engage any talent scouts. Serious talent development when all's said and done is part of the corporate strategy, or it's not. If it's not, then the company should not keep saying over and over again that it is. But *if* it is, then investments should be made to make sure the company survives and prospers.

Innovation is every company's lifeblood. But as with lots of essential activities that get lost in a crisis, innovation is underfunded. Given the political realities of the global economic crisis, we need to be creative about how we spend time, effort, and money to keep innovation alive. Nothing is "free," but there are any number of relatively low-cost, low-risk innovation investments that can be made in high-potential innovation initiatives that can be sold internally as important and even cost effective. I have discussed a number of low-cost, low-risk, high-impact opportunities. There are many others. Find them; seize them. Because when all this settles down, and it will, we'll all need to innovate again.

TOUGH LOVE BUSINESS CASES

Everyone has a perspective on return on investment. As discussed at the beginning of this chapter, there are lots of calculations, models, and algorithms that allegedly measure precisely the impact of alternative technology investments. There is strategic ROI and tactical ROI; there is "soft" ROI and "hard" ROI. There are as many ROIs out there as there are RBIs in the major leagues. What do we make of the ROI smorgasbord? Let's look at the targets of our return-on-investment analyses, not on the methods, tools, and techniques. In other words, let's ask the unconventional questions.

Tough Love

Web 2.0 is very hot; even Web 3.0 (whatever that is) is catching fire. Will these technologies help your business save money or make money? Will they help you comply? What about service-oriented architecture (SOA)? What about software-as-a-service? What about your people? What about your organizational structure? Even your business strategy: what's working? What's not?

How tough should we be? Very. The fact is that much of our technology is barely vetted and that we often simply don't know what the returns on our investments really are. So let's step back and ask some tough questions about some questionable technologies, and people, organizations, and strategies.

Web 2.0

Web 2.0 technologies, such as wikis, blogs, RSS filters, mashups, podcasts, folksonomies, crowdsourcing, social networks, and virtual worlds, are very hot. Everyone is excited about deploying them, especially because they're fast and cheap. But what do they really deliver?

There are at least six impact areas:

- Knowledge management (KM)
- Rapid application development (RAD)
- Customer relationship management (CRM)
- Collaboration and communication
- Innovation
- Training

The issues are simple: what is the impact that Web 2.0 technologies are having on these six areas? The first phase of our research indicates that the answer is: "not much." It turns out that the early applications of Web 2.0

technologies are ambiguous at best.* What does this tell us? First, it tells us that hype always precedes impact. It also tells us that performance metrics must be part of every business case to pilot new technologies. Cool is fun but not cost effective.

It also tells us that vendors, trade publications, overeager technology managers, and cocktail-drinking CEOs often become intoxicated by the promise of new technologies and prematurely invest in what they expect will be boffo results. Is no one immune? There are definitely executives who hate everything; I can still remember a CFO of a Fortune 50 company telling his senior management team (SMT) in the late 1990s that the Internet was a fad that would be gone in two years. Yes, he (not so) secretly hated technology but because he controlled the technology budget was able to seriously undermine the company's ability to compete in the late twentieth and early twenty-first century (he retired wealthy and now travels the world avoiding hotels with Internet access). But there are many executives susceptible to technology hype, especially if it's wrapped in a competitive threat: I have always found it easier to get the attention of SMTs when I discuss the competition. How the competition is using technology is always an interesting topic.

You must communicate an ROI strategy that's meaningful to the company. The troops need to understand that their company is smart and careful, not stupid and reckless. After all, this stuff costs a lot of money. Proactivity here is essential: keeping quiet contributes to the emperor-has-no-clothes syndrome. The SMT must get out in front of the technology adoption strategy, communicate it exhaustively, and then walk the walk.

ALTERNATIVE DELIVERY MODELS

Sourcing now comes in all flavors. We can rent hardware, software, communications, storage, and entire infrastructures. We can outsource to vendors down the street or across the globe. Salesforce.com pioneered the

---

* See Steve Andriole, "Wikis, Blogs, Podcasts, Mashups, Folksonomies, RSS Filters, Social Networks, Virtual Worlds & Crowdsourcing for Corporate Productivity & Management: Early Impact Assessments & Undeniable Trends," the Cutter Consortium, August 2008.

software-as-a-service delivery model as IBM branded "on-demand." But do they all work?

The tough business case begins with performance metrics for the current delivery model. If you don't have them, it will be impossible to assess the impact that alternative delivery models will have on business performance. But wait! There are other metrics that must be considered, metrics that are often hidden or disguised. Maybe the company would like to outsource because it has decided that technology is no longer a core competency. Maybe it has decided to adopt SaaS and hardware-as-a-service because it believes that it can save a lot of money. Or maybe it just wants to try something new to convince a potential acquirer that "there's nothing stale about this company!" Whatever the motivation, we need to specify and quantify the metrics that define the strategic and tactical objectives of the company.

The delivery models based on renting versus building and deploying must be evaluated carefully. Current performance metrics + objectives + alternative delivery model metrics = impact. Piloting the models makes perfect sense; enterprise rollouts without pilots are insane. Baby steps make more sense than Herculean leaps.

PEOPLE

People are the strongest—and (mostly the) weakest—link. Are your people any good? How do you know? When was the last time you did a skills gap analysis? Most of the CIOs and CTOs we speak with do not have a handle on the skills of their staffs. The way to assess your staff is to juxtapose the current and future computing and communications requirements with current and future skill sets. But the real work lies in the objective assessment of the gaps between what you will need and what you will have. The sad fact is that nearly all companies underinvest in the development of their professionals, which inevitably results in skills gaps. Assess what the company is doing about closing the gaps. Are there internal and external training programs? Are they making a difference? Are there "before" and "after" metrics to determine if training and education are effective? Are incentives in place to reward and punish employees who achieve and underachieve? I talked about this in Chapter 2. You might want to reread Chapter 2 now.

ORGANIZATIONS

Are you organized effectively? Do you have the right people reporting to the right people doing the right things? Is your governance explicit? Do you have the right centralization:decentralization ratio? Is there accountability? Is the organization flexible? Most important, is the organization perceived by its customers as effective? Perhaps the most important metric is what the user community thinks of its technology organization. A serious objective assessment of how the technology organization is perceived is job one. Companies need to know where the technology organization sits in the corporate hierarchy. Is it respected? Disrespected? Ridiculed? Openly mocked? Is the help desk frequently referred to as the helpless desk? In interviews we've conducted over the past few years, we've found that technology organizations think they are performing better than any of their customers, who often think they are slow, expensive, sometimes arrogant, and incapable of managing complex projects. It's essential to objectively profile the technology organization.

STRATEGY

Can you find your company's business strategy? Is it comprised of specific models and processes? Does it reference the conventional and unconventional competition? Is it taken seriously by the senior management team? Is it properly funded? Vet the strategy. How sound is it? How persistent is it? Is there a correlation between what is published and what is practiced? Strategy metrics are complicated and usually ignored because—surprise— strategies are often political documents written for internal consumption, investors, and advertisers.

Assessing corporate strategies is complicated and political, but necessary to understand if a company is rudderless or focused. Beware of companies that have disjointed strategies but high expectations about the contributions that technology can make to its ability to make money or save money.

TECHNOLOGY ADOPTION—ONE MORE TIME

How many times will we dissect the early-to-late technology adoption curve? How should we manage broken adoption processes and unreasonable expectations? First, you need to look and act like the professional you can be. You need to own the adoption curve. You need to distinguish between technologies that are ripe and those that are still growing on the vine. Is this hard to do? Not for seasoned technology professionals who can not only make the distinction but also communicate the try-before-buy approach to mature technology adoption. Why would anyone advocate an alternative approach?

ROI is about tough choices and tough questions. Much ROI analysis is staged and mechanistic. The argument here is to focus on truly meaningful outcomes, concentrating less on the methodology and much more on the objective metrics that matter. And we all know what the most important metrics look like.

FINAL THOUGHTS ABOUT MANAGEMENT

This chapter is all over the place because management is all over the place, and then some. Managers make decisions. They track technology and business trends and exploit the intersection.

The key today is to challenge all of the assumptions about how to acquire, deploy, and support technology that we believed worked for decades. The fact is that we were in a 30-year prototyping project that has finally yielded some actionable results: TCO and ROI are not weapons, but opportunities. Risk is more about the cost of inaction than the poor execution of high-risk projects. The toughest business cases should apply to the highest potential technologies. You can do innovative things quickly and cheaply. You can begin all this with an audit that benchmarks your current state and describes your future state. Get on with the business of organic management.

4

Sourcing

This chapter looks at the delivery of digital technology. Is there anything new to add here? Sorry to shock you, but there are at least 15 new "alternative" technology delivery models out there; the Gartner Group just cannot control itself. Nor can the other industry research companies that make money by convincing you that what you believe is just wrong, or at best incomplete.

But the fact is that there are alternatives in the mix that change the sourcing game. For example, imagine if companies no longer provided PCs or smart phones to their employees. Imagine if they moved everything to the cloud. Imagine if they adopted open-source software wherever they could.

The X-as-a-service revolution is gathering lots of steam and makes lots of sense for a lot of companies who never should have been in the technology business in the first place. The industry is finally providing the means for companies to escape the control, inflexibility, and cost of traditional delivery models. What took so long? And why are companies still waffling about their effectiveness? Sure, I like pilots, but they should be assessed around why the new delivery models don't work rather than searching endlessly for perfect performance metrics.

Vendor management must move to the next level. As I've already discussed in this book several times, vendor management is the new core competency, replacing server farm operations. The number of companies that will run their own infrastructures will decrease year after year until they're all gone. Only the Luddites will remain, running operations for the Flat Earth Society.

The chapter begins with the inevitable: that more and more outsourcing is inevitable, but not for the reasons you might think. The chapter ends with a 10-step process to change the way you acquire, deploy, and support digital technology. IT's all done but the shouting (and the development of solid SLAs).

WHY MORE (AND MORE AND MORE) OUTSOURCING IS INEVITABLE

Time for an outsourcing reality check. Everyone's excited about how well or poorly outsourcing works, so let's take a look at what's happening now, and what's likely to happen over the next few years. Let me say first that much of the fate around outsourcing has already been sealed. I realize that there are reports that near- and off-shore outsourcing deals do not save as much money as many people assumed. Some reports suggest that quality is a continuing problem, and others complain about language barriers, competing processes, and the management challenges that especially plague many off-shore outsourcing projects. But the fate is sealed.

First, the number of management information systems (MIS), information systems (IS), computer science (CS), and computer engineering (CE) majors in the United States has fallen so dramatically that we're likely to lose an entire generation of replacement technologists if present trends continue, and they show every sign of doing so. So as the previous generation continues to gray, there will be precious few new technologists to keep the skills pipeline full. The obvious outcome is increased demand for the skills, wherever they happen to be.

A second trend that will fuel the demand for more outsourcing is standardization and its cousin commoditization. The industry is making increasingly less variant stuff work together. Although web services and service-oriented architectures (SOAs) represent impressive technology they also represent freedom to those who deploy and support technology. Vendor consolidation is also fueling standardization and commoditization, and if you believe the impact that SOAs will have on software development, support, and licensing, the stage is set for the massive decentralization of cooperative software components. If this playing field truly levels itself out, the door will open even farther for outsourcers who will master the new architectures (as a natural extension from where they are now in applications development and integration).

The third trend to watch is "the end of corporate computing," or the desire to buy services and rent applications rather than deploy and support them in-house. Initially, companies will purchase transaction-processing services from centralized data centers managed by large technology providers, but over time companies will rent applications developed the old-fashioned way by the same old mega software vendors. But eventually, as

SOA proliferates, new software delivery and support models will develop from the old vendors as well as a host of new ones: "hosting" applications will yield to "assembling" applications. The appeal of "paying by the drink" is just too great to resist, especially because the alternative will still (and forever) require the care and feeding of increasingly difficult to find technology professionals.

If you look at these trends there's plenty of reason to believe that down-the-street, near-shore, and off-shore outsourcing will all increase over the next few years and certainly, as I believe, even more in the next decade. The recent backlash that describes failed or too-expensive outsourcing deals, although in many cases is absolutely justified, will be crushed by the inevitability that the above three trends, among others, will create. All of these trends are important; however, I think the most troubling one is the technology-avoidance strategy practiced by so many undergraduates today. It's as if they've all but given up on technology careers, believing instead that they're better off studying accounting, communications, or history. (At least the history majors can help us understand what happened to the U.S. technology market in the early twenty-first century.)

VENDORS, VENDORS, EVERYWHERE

Many of us see vendors as necessary evils. We need PCs and laptops so we grudgingly write an RFP to begin what we dread as the unpleasant selection process. We feel the same way about negotiating enterprise software licenses, desktop support contracts, and wireless communications. We know we need the stuff, but we really don't like the acquisition process. What's going on here?

Technologists (and their acquisition teams) who see vendors as necessary evils are short-sighted and sometimes, well, just plain lazy. The necessary evil perspective is really very 1980s and doesn't reflect even late twentieth-century thinking about technology optimization. If you're in this camp, you might want to rethink your approach to acquisition, deployment, and support. If your vendors are necessary evils then by definition you'll minimize contact with them and your interest in their offerings. You will keep them at arm's length and ultimately fail to integrate business and technology.

But things could be worse. Some of us see vendors as adversaries who should be defeated every time we get the chance. There may be some valid reasons for hating vendors (there are always valid reasons for hating professionals with whom we contend); there are few if any valid reasons to hold grudges, lose perspective, or otherwise make emotional decisions that hurt our companies (and the vendors we hate). If you find it impossible to deal with a vendor for ethical reasons replace the vendor, don't try to kill him. The vendors-as-adversaries approach wastes way too much energy on the wrong things. About all it's good for is generating bragging rights at two o'clock in the bar.

Vendors are not always trouble. In fact, the smart play as we move toward business technology synergism is to develop wide and deep relationships with vendors that link directly to key business metrics such as cost management, growth, and profitability. In fact, just as we think about the ROI of technology projects we should think about tactical and strategic ROI of our vendor relationships. Do we really need the data warehouse guys who charge us an arm and a leg? How dependent are we on our ERP (enterprise resource planning) implementation/integration/support vendor? Heavily? OK, then let's make that vendor a strategic partner. Let's let that vendor "in" to participate in our strategic planning and the delivery of our products and services.

The subset of vendors that have measurable tactical and strategic value is probably smaller than you think, but the value of the group may be much greater than you realize. The vendors that make the short list should be invited into your inner circle. In return for a long-term business commitment, they will ride the highs and lows of your business. They will understand your requirements and try as hard as they possibly can not to shamelessly exploit this understanding. They will help finance your technology purchases, with favorable terms, in exchange for a long-term business commitment. Under the umbrella of professional although not oppressive nondisclosure agreements you will share information, insights, and plans. This will permit you to optimize their contributions to your business.

Bite the bullet and look for partners you can control. The technology industry is consolidating. In five years there will be only several players in each major space. Already, we're essentially down to three enterprise database vendors and a few networking and communications vendors. How many ERP vendors are there likely to be in three years? The boundaries around transaction processing are also changing. It's impossible to strategize your business around sets of discrete disconnected events, or the vendors that support them. Instead, business is becoming continuous and the vendors that support 24/7 transaction processing simply cannot be organized as a horde of adversaries that are, one hopes, all perfectly incentivized to do exactly what you want when you want it (at the right price). The macro trends in our industry validate the search for good partners even if (or should I say, especially if) they're vendors.

HAS ANYONE BEEN TO NORDSTROM?

One morning I spent some time (a lot of time, actually) on hold with and occasionally actually speaking to "technical support" representatives from Dell.* Six months ago, I purchased a pretty spiffy Dell desktop. I listened to the on-hold voice tell me over and over again that I could just go to Dell.com for technical support, because the scripts that the organic technical support team used to troubleshoot problems were the same scripts that the digital technical support team used. This advice struck me as peculiar: if I could really get the answers I needed from the web then why was Dell spending so much money frustrating me with 800-number support? Was the voice implying that I was an idiot to actually want to speak with someone? I bounced from service rep to service rep, ending with a (live) Dell support professional telling me that she did not know how to solve my problem. (My DVD player quits every time I try to play a DVD, not exactly a world-class problem.†) She walked me through the troubleshooting scripts, we reinstalled drivers, and so on, but nothing worked.

What I experienced was the worst of all worlds. After several hours of annoying music, and after being rerouted five times, it occurred to me that maybe we haven't come all that far, at least in the computer industry, with customer service. This assessment was punctuated by my being told that if the problem was a software problem, I would be charged a fee for the help, even though I paid for three years of support (learning during the service

---

* In fact, I wrote this while on hold with Dell.
† I subsequently posted a message to a community board only to discover that lots of people have the same problem; I got some good tips on how to solve the problem from perfect strangers who were happy to receive a "thank you" as payment for their services. Maybe they worked for Nordstroms during the day.

experience that my warranty only covered hardware) or I could call the software manufacturer myself to discuss my problem.

The experience with Dell was redefined after an experience with the Nordstrom retail chain. I find it hard to imagine a Nordstrom service representative telling me that I had to contact the manufacturer of the shirt whose sleeves were falling off because Nordstrom only supports the boxes in which the shirts are sold, or if I wanted the shirt repaired or replaced, I'd have to pay an additional fee or take a trip abroad to solve my problem. If you've shopped at Nordstrom you know that there's essentially nothing they cannot do for you: the customer is—literally—always right.

Do you pay more for this service? Of course. Truly excellent service is embedded in the purchase price, and for those who want to make the price/service trade-off, the rewards are clear. Dell of course is not the only vendor whose "support" is far from perfect. In fact, given that Dell (and other hardware and software vendors) worries more about being cheap than supported, when one buys a Dell one should expect to receive the same service as one would receive at K-Mart or Walmart, inasmuch as these chains are often the low-cost retail provider: it would cost Dell, and therefore us, way too much to provide Nordstrom-like support at K-Mart or any retail chain that guarantees low prices every day.

So how should the industry deal with complexity, support ambiguities, ineffective customer service, and service loopholes? As a customer, I think it's simple: as long as desktop and laptop operating systems and applications software are so complex, the product of so many different vendors, and subject to so many failures and conflicts, whoever sells the (hardware + software) system should be responsible for supporting what they sell. They should not be able to point a finger somewhere else, charge for fixing problems that are bundled in their own branded boxes, or cut customers loose to solve problems on their own. Is there another retail industry that treats its customers this way? Only the low-cost ones. So what do we want? Cheap prices or great support? Yes.

All of this explains why desktop/laptop support is one of the fastest growing outsourcing targets and why technology consultants for personal residences are popping up all over the place. We all need more help with fewer headaches. If I manufactured the hardware and software, I'd try to interrupt these trends; I'd try to own my customers.

TECHNOLOGY LIFE IN THE CLOUDS

Not too many years ago when we invested in start-up technology companies we'd set aside about 10% to 15% of the funds we raised for the technology infrastructure. This was a high percentage of funds going to PCs, servers, and software, especially when every dollar was precious and necessary for marketing, product development, and, of course, sales. Fast-forward a decade or so and the cost is now 1% to 5%. Most start-ups buy nothing, install nothing, and support as little as possible. What's going on? CAPEX is gone and expensing is in: companies pay by the drink from the corner bar, or the one that's a continent away. Almost 10 years ago we looked to application service providers (ASPs, remember them?) to satisfy our drinking desires. Now we turn to all kinds of providers who will host and rent just about anything. Software-as-a-service (SaaS) + hardware-as-a-service (HaaS) = technology independence, or at least freedom from operational technology.

We are on the cusp of a major shift in the delivery of information technology. Although we can expect start-ups to lead the way, mid-sized companies have also discovered the joys of technology independence. Even large enterprises are looking to the clouds for help. But before I get too far into the SWOT analysis of cloud computing, let's define some terms. Wikipedia defines "the cloud" as:

> Cloud computing provides computation, software, data access, and storage services that do not require end-user knowledge of the physical location and configuration of the system that delivers the services. Parallels to this concept can be drawn with the electricity grid, wherein end-users consume power without needing to understand the component devices or infrastructure required to provide the service.
>
> Cloud computing describes a new supplement, consumption, and delivery model for IT services based on Internet protocols, and it typically involves provisioning of dynamically scalable and often virtualized resources. It is a byproduct and consequence of the ease-of-access to remote computing sites provided by the Internet. This may take the form of web-based tools or applications that users can access and use through a web browser as if they were programs installed locally on their computer.
>
> Cloud computing providers deliver applications via the internet, which are accessed from a web browser, while the business software and data are stored on servers at a remote location. In some cases, legacy applications

(line of businss applications that until now have been prevalent in thin client Windows computing) are delivered via a screen-sharing technology such as Citix XenApp, while the computing resources are consolidated at a remote data center location; in oher cases, entire business applications have been coded using web-based technologies such as AJAX.

Most cloud computing infrastructure consist of services delivered through shared data-centers and appearing as a single point of access for consumers' computing needs. Commercial offerings may be required to meet service level agreements (SLAs), but specific terms are less often http://en.wikipedia.org/wiki/Cloud_computing.

The SO part of the SWOT (strengths, weaknesses, opportunities, and threats) equation (at least as I've rewritten it here) is multidimensional. First and foremost is the shift in philosophy that occurs when companies start pondering how they might exploit cloud computing. As already suggested, small and mid-sized companies have embraced cloud computing for several reasons, including cost, flexibility, and the desire to define operational technology as a minor, if any, part of their core competency. Larger companies have also taken the plunge (or jumped into the ether) usually in pieces: a little SaaS here, a little HaaS there.

One of the major strengths of cloud computing is the freedom it provides companies to think strategically, not tactically, about how they want to leverage technology. Instead of worrying about network latency and server maintenance, business technology professionals can focus on innovation, sales, and marketing, among other revenue-generating activities. Another strength is flexibility. Picking from a menu is easier than designing one. Scalability is often just a phone call or e-mail away. The freedom from software maintenance, denial-of-service attacks, viruses, and other operational headaches is also a byproduct of cloud computing.

There are also clear cost savings. When done right, cloud computing can save companies significant money over the years. As a rule of thumb, I tell my clients, for example, that the cost savings they should expect is in the 25% to 33% range depending, again, on the nature of the infrastructure, the number of users, and the number of applications put to work.

There's comfort in bigness. When IBM branded itself as the "on-demand" company it was anticipating cloud computing. We all know how many CIOs and CTOs hide under the credibility umbrella of IBM (and other big vendors that have embraced cloud computing and on-demand service offerings). Had the major technology vendors not endorsed the approach, there would have been problems with the whole delivery model. But instead they went the other way; at least many of them did (some of the old-time enterprise software vendors are still clinging to their annual enterprise licensing fees and may do so until they crash and burn).

The WT part of the equation is tricky. As with all new delivery models there are hiccups and landmines. The hiccups still largely have to do with access to reliable fast networks that keep everyone connected to the cloud and its data, applications, and communications technology. "Always on" takes on added importance in cloud computing, where the phrase literally must mean "always on." There are also issues around pricing (pay-by-the-drink versus subscriptions versus hybrids), configuration, and service.

The landmines are real. There are security risks that must be managed. The entry of IBM, Google, and AT&T, among other major providers, into the cloud computing market has relieved some of the pressure here but there are still lots of CIOs and CTOs (spurred by their cautious business colleagues) worried about vulnerabilities and liabilities, especially if the cloud provider relies upon other providers, as many of them do: executives are especially sensitive to delivery models with multiple points of failure.

There are also philosophical weaknesses. Some companies just cannot accept the idea that their data, applications, transactions, and even hardware are somewhere else, owned and operated by strangers. I must confess that I never understood this logic. Anytime I hear this reaction to cloud computing I ask the complainer if there's any outsourcing going on at the company. Turns out that IBM is often running the data centers and Deloitte or Accenture is supporting their ERP applications and all kinds of outsiders are running telecommunications: just about everyone is already outsourcing some part of the infrastructure. That said, there is still resistance to the perceived dependence on the cloud. What if it crashes? What if hackers take it down? What if someone steals my data? What if I change my mind and want to leave the cloud? Although these are all good questions, there are some pretty good answers to them, assuming that you are philosophically inclined to even go into the cloud.

I say "tomahtoes" and you say "tomaytoes"; I say "ant" and you say "ahnt." The world is comprised of very different people with different technology acquisition, deployment, and support biases. Some companies will never enter the cloud; many will enter it only after just about everyone thoroughly tests the air; and some will actually enter it today. My sense is that core competency is driving the decision to enter or not. Companies that want to get completely out of the operational technology business eventually will enter the cloud as early as possible; companies that cling to operational (and strategic) technology as part of their core competency will avoid the cloud.

The larger questions are about the Internet itself and, ultimately, what it can and cannot do. There are some serious issues around the Internet's architecture. Some believe it's on the verge of collapse, whereas others believe that it's only a few thousand servers away from stability. The United States has not made the Internet part of the national infrastructure. Depending on what you think about government efficiency, you may want to keep the government as far away as possible from the policies and technologies of the Internet and the World Wide Web. But just as wireless device adoption was gaited by the speed of wireless networks, so too will the adoption of cloud computing be driven by the Internet's overall stability, reliability, scalability, and security. Its capabilities must be assured by someone or lots of potential cloud computers will stay away.

So what's life like in the cloud? Here are some trends:

- The cloud's offerings will only expand; more and more applications and transactions will live in the cloud.
- The cloud will become the engine of transaction-processing innovation, where open-source components will be published much more frequently than any of the newspapers or magazines we read. They will also be "certified" and cleaned for mashups, interoperability, and quick fixes.
- More and more companies will offer comprehensive cloud services; even the stubborn proprietary enterprise software vendors will come around.
- Technology will become less and less of a core competency for more and more companies: why buy (support, upgrade) when you can lease? Although the principle may not hold for houses and even automobiles, it certainly does for technology infrastructures and architectures.
- New cost models for technology delivery will be driven by cloud computing. More and more companies will figure out how to deliver more and more services for less and less money. The cloud will trigger whole new competitive pricing models: all good for consumers.

WHAT START-UPS AND WIND-DOWNS DO NOW

Figure 4.1 (which you've seen before) about sums it up. We don't need to hear from Nick Carr (*IT Doesn't Matter*; *The Big Switch*); we don't need another industry briefing or even the guys on CNBC talking about the sea change called Google. The industry was moving long before all of these smart people learned how to monetize the trend with catchy phrases, titles, and insights. (Yes, I am jealous that I didn't coin a phrase like "IT Doesn't Matter.") Figure 4.1 summarizes the trends that many of us in the business saw a long time ago, especially right after the nuclear winter of 2000 (when the Y2K problem embarrassed the field with its timidity and technology spending cratered).

Figure 4.1 reflects the massive shift in platforms over the past 30 years. We're moving outside the corporate firewall into "the cloud." So what does this mean for start-ups and wind-downs?

Start-Up Tactics

Let's assume that you leave your company, grab a couple of buddies, and decide to launch a new company. After all, it has to be easier than what you're doing at the ranch, right? How do you acquire, deploy, and support the technology you'll need to operate your business?

The important difference here is the lack of existing infrastructure, legacy applications, disparate databases, and long-term outsourcing deals

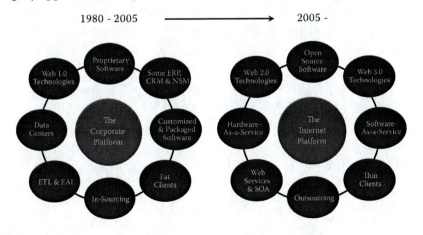

FIGURE 4.1
Off to a new era.

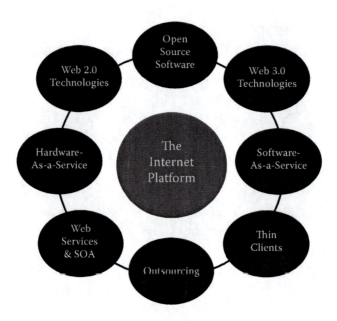

FIGURE 4.2
Start-up compass.

that might still be breathing, albeit probably on life support. You're free to start fresh, to strategize without constraints. What should you do? Figure 4.2 is your compass.

Your first decision focuses on proprietary versus open-source software. Do you need any proprietary software? You can avoid Microsoft Office, Oracle/Siebel CRM, and countless other expensive applications. Better still, you can rent them all—e-mail, workflow, CRM, database management, among so many others—and not even care about whether the software is open-source-based or from some proprietary vintage.

Software-as-a-service could become one of your best friends as you try to avoid the care and feeding of multiple software applications. SaaS is not just for e-mail, workflow, or CRM. Enterprise resource planning applications can be rented as easily as business intelligence (BI) applications. If I'm lucky I will find a reliable provider who will rent me a suite of open-source applications that are even cheaper than paying by the drink for proprietary applications. Functionality will drive my decision making, not brand names. Sure, Siebel CRM sounds better than SugarCRM, but do I care about the name? How many people laughed at the name "Google" when it first appeared? If it were me, I would absolutely deploy thin clients. Why do I need fat clients running all kinds of bloatware? Thin clients provide the ability completely to avoid break-and-fix headaches, expensive software upgrades, and even virus penetration. I can give them out like candy and forget about "maintaining" or "upgrading" them. My God, why didn't I think about this before? The answer, of course, is that communications networks were not robust or secure enough to support thin client architectures, but they are now. I cannot imagine an entrepreneur handing out heavy Wintel monsters to his employees. I'd just give them all light thin clients with continuous network access to software and database applications that sit on servers managed by trusted third-party providers.

Do I need a data center? Probably, but I can rent the hardware from any number of vendors. Even better: I can hire a managed service provider to run my data center (with rented hardware and software). I will assume behind-the-curtain interoperability via the industry's improving standardization of interfaces and the formalization of service-oriented and event-driven architectures (EDA), but do I really care how integration and interoperability happen? Web 2.0 and Web 3.0 technologies provide opportunities for me to deepen the collaboration among employees, partners, customers, and suppliers. I can talk to these people in all sorts of ways through all sorts of channels and portals, including blogs and wikis. I can even interact with them in virtual reality. Folksonomies help me organize and find data; really simple syndication (RSS) filters help me deliver the right information to the right people at the right time. Mashups help me build rich applications really fast; they are today's rapid prototypes. Crowdsourcing offers me a way to put lots of minds to work on the array of problems haunting me at any particular time. I get to leverage the "wisdom of the crowd," which is far from perfect, of course, whenever I like. If I really get creative I can devise contests in which the crowd participates, paying generous cash prizes for superior performance.

So where does my start-up technology live? "In the cloud," as they say, but obviously not inside my firewall because I don't have a firewall! I forfeited control, centralization, and even standardization for agility, flexibility, and mobility. If I do all this right, I should be paying less than if I had a firewall and kept everything inside it.

Wind-Down Tactics

There are so many attitudes, perceptions, and "best practices" that have to change to wind down corporate computing as it once was. The drag of concepts such as control, standardization, single source (versus best of breed), and centralization can really limit progress toward the new era. This is not to say that all these concepts are bad. Standardization of network access devices, for example, is a sound best practice, but which access devices should be standardized? Similarly, the centralization of infrastructure can make sense, but how and where should it be housed, and who should house it?

How do legacy companies with legacy technology environments exploit open-source software? Do they really want to, or are they committed to their proprietary partners? How do you develop the business case for alternative software providers? Can you send the crown jewels down the street or across the globe for safe keeping? Or will you worry every night about where they really are, what they're doing, and who's wearing them?

The real challenge for legacy companies (represented in Figure 4.3) is liberation from past habits, values, business cases, hardware, software, processes, and services. The idea, for example, of importing widgets, APIs, and other tools from the web to develop or extend applications scares the hell out of many CIOs and CTOs. If these technology managers are over 50 years of age, the idea could be fatal. Existing capital investments in technology also constrain CIOs and CTOs interested in the new era. The way we've paid for and depreciated technology affects the way we monetize

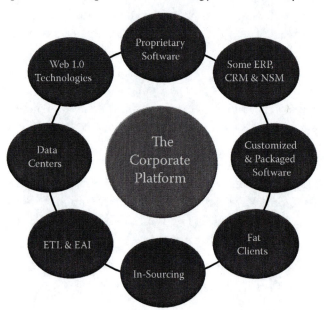

FIGURE 4.3
Wind-down constraints.

its value. If everything were expensed annually, there would be different attitudes about what to buy, lease, rent, or decommission. Clearly, moving to the cloud is a journey toward expensing technology costs.

But the real issue at many companies is control. The consumerization of technology propels herds of cats out of the bag. What will things be like when the next wave of professionals graduates and invades the workforce? Who writes the rules will become as important as the rules themselves.

Why does anyone pay maintenance fees for proprietary software that sits inside the firewall behind armed corporate guards (also known as database administrators and software developers)? We've gone from customized applications to packaged applications and many of us are pretty happy with this arrangement, especially the consultants who make a fortune installing and supporting proprietary packaged software applications.

Fat clients? Time to put them all on crash diets. Legacy companies maintain way too much of their domain knowledge, business processes, and data on fat clients that travel the world largely unsupervised. Security breaches are becoming commonplace. So what if the data didn't sit on network access devices? Detoxing from the Wintel addiction will be initially painful, but ultimately cost effective and secure.

Winding down also means rethinking the sourcing arrangements that legacy companies have in place. Sure, they've outsourced the help desk. Big deal. Many companies agonized for years over simple outsourcing decisions such as support: we can do it better ... no we can't ... cheaper ... maybe not ... knowledge transfer, that's the ticket ... no, wait, no one wants to transfer help desk knowledge.

Data integration? Yes, of course, they say, we have (proprietary) enterprise application integration (EAI) tools that we bought a few years ago. They still work pretty well, so we'll keep using them. Sure, service-oriented architecture is important to us, but we get it mostly from our vendors that embed it in their software updates.

Our data centers are impenetrable! We've invested millions in security, back-up, and recovery. We get terrific yields from our server farms. We're solid here. We know how to manage a data center. Which, of course, is the problem: many companies have gotten really good at doing things that matter less and less. Time to rethink the hardware.

OK, so your use of the web is really very 1.0. What would you have us do? For starters, move as many transactions as possible onto the web. Think of the web as a legitimate scalable channel that you get to pretty much control. Help your suppliers, partners, and customers collaborate with you and among themselves through your corporate portal, which also needs windows into the clouds that surround it.

Legacy companies also often need a people-cleaning. Age affects problem solving. Age drives perspective and preferences. Aging seeks the path of least resistance or, put another way, avoids change. Is John McCain "too old"? Is Barack Obama "too young"? Think about the relationship between age and change. Is it strong enough to affect an organization's ability to progress? If the average age of the technology community in a twenty-first-century company is well over 40, moving across platforms will be difficult if not impossible to do. I realize that no one wants to hear this kind of argument, but if large amounts of time are spent discussing old application projects, hardware, or the good ol' days then you've got a serious problem. It's important to manage the gap between the youngest and oldest technology professionals. If the gap grows too wide too fast, you will have to manage a nasty "two cultures" problem, something you want to avoid at all cost.

All of this used to be about core competencies. Just five years ago we'd all sit around and debate the merits of being in the technology business and the merits of outsourcing it all away. It's no longer just about core competency; now it's about competing. The Internet platform is the springboard to speed, agility, security, and reliability; the old corporate platform is about control, centralization, and maintenance. Moving from one platform to the other will ultimately become more of a management challenge than a technology one.

SOURCING, SOURCING EVERYWHERE

The appeal of outsourcing is still cost savings and, increasingly, discipline in the form of elegant software documentation and improved reliability (in the case of software development and systems integration) and efficient processes and excellent customer and employee interaction (in the case of call centers). Everything's a candidate for outsourcing it seems: front-office, back-office, and virtual-office tasks are all on the list: you can always find someone to do whatever you need them to do, for a price, of course. But before you leap into a short-term or (especially) long-term outsourcing agreement, you need to know some things.

First, you need to know how to craft a diagnostic outsourcing request for proposal (RFP). The most important aspect of this process is the width and depth of your understanding of the work you want to relinquish: if you don't fully understand what you want an outsourcer to do, the deal will explode. The incarnation of this understanding will be your RFP of the tasks to be performed, and the details of the service-level agreement (SLA) you'll want the outsourcer to honor. These documents need to be works of art, but don't expect elegant pieces of paper to actually manage the arrangement. You'll have to do this personally.

Second, you need to know what should stay close to home and what you can export to India, the Philippines, Ireland, Russia, or wherever. Companies have outsourced technology and business processes to a variety of companies outside the United States in order to save money and improve quality. When tasks are well-defined and repeatable, and when you know a lot about them, they can be exported. When the outsourcing deal is with a company thousands of miles away it had better be well conceived and well oiled: outsource far from home only when you understand the processes and objectives, have a mutually beneficial explicit service-level agreement, and metrics that enable you to track performance at least quarterly (I actually prefer monthly tracking).

Third, you need to know how to develop contingency plans, and the more distant the partner, the more robust the plans should be. I understand that ubiquitous communications shrink distance and time, but we should never underestimate the need for hands-on, face-to-face management, especially hands-on, face-to-face crisis management. If an off-shore outsourcing effort is extremely strategic to your company, you should consider opening an office near your partner to stay close to progress and problems.

Fourth, you need to tap into insight about social and political climates in the countries and regions where you have outsourcing partners. It's obviously a volatile world, and it's possible to have great partners who find themselves held hostage to paralyzing economic, political, and military events: do you want to be the champion of outsourcing deals to countries whose economic and political systems are fragile, or whose military enemies are formidable, and close?

Fifth, be completely honest with yourself (and management) about the total cost of outsourcing. The essential tasks—coding, answering phones, processing checks, and the like—may be much cheaper, but there are all sorts of additional costs that must be calculated, costs such as additional travel, additional management, on-site presence, and performance monitoring. So-called "soft costs" will also kill you here. Model all of the hard, soft, and other costs before you outsource, and then again during and after the outsourcing experience.

Finally, you need to keep asking tough questions about your current and anticipated core competencies. Why are you outsourcing? By this time, you should know that just saving money is sometimes a horrible reason to outsource anything. Outsourcing decisions should be driven by objective assessments about what it is you do well (and poorly), cost effectively (and too expensively), what you think your competitive differentiators are (and will be), and what you really want your company to be (and not be) going forward. One more thing: try as hard as you can to keep the politics as quiet as possible when you're making important outsourcing decisions, especially decisions that will land a continent away. Outsourcing can often make perfect sense. But it can sometimes result in hideous outcomes. Be careful out there.

NEW WAYS TO DELIVER OLD SERVICES FOR LESS MONEY

The economic times present us with unique opportunities to change people, processes, and technology. We thought we saw it all after the dot-com crash. The nuclear winter that persisted from 2000–2003 taught us some tough lessons about how volatile technology spending can be. When we emerged from the "end of the world" in 2004, we felt confident about the future of technology spending, that it would be more balanced and predictable going forward. We, of course, were wrong. By late 2008 all bets were once again off. 2009 and 2010 looked even worse. CIOs and CTOs receive memoranda ordering them to dramatically reduce technology spending. CAPEX projects are on hold (if not dead forever) and companies are looking for ways to cut costs any way they can. Nothing is off the table.

Just as all this is unfolding, the field is offering a variety of alternative technology delivery methods and processes. Many of these predate the economic crisis even by several years, but many of them are being refined in real time as the need to save money accelerates. Five of the more prominent ones are based on:

- Open-source software
- Web 2.0 technologies
- Hardware-as-a-service
- Software-as-a-service
- Thin client architecture

There are others. Storage-as-a-service, communications-as-a-service, and bring-your-computer-to-work programs are also being assessed for their ability to reduce costs while preserving services.

The larger issue is process and technology adoption. Alternative delivery models and new business technology processes are usually vetted over time with a series of demonstration pilots intended to define value, impact, and risk, the proverbial elements of an investment business case. CIOs and CTOs, often conservative by nature, carefully examine alternatives before adopting technologies or processes.

The cross-pressures around adoption, saving money, and deliberate due diligence are colliding. Conservative technologists are under extraordinary pressure to reduce their budgets. This is a true conundrum for management. The wild card is the new delivery models that sit in the middle of these classic decision-making drivers.

As these issues play out, companies are already altering their sourcing strategies. The larger question is to what extent are these alterations permanent or temporary? As we know from previous trends, outsourcing momentum is its own stimulus. Many of the alterations could well be permanent, especially as the industry continues to offer alternative cost-effective sourcing options. In fact, the need to reduce costs is likely to become an even more permanent sourcing driver even when the immediate economic crisis subsides. Figure 4.4 sets the stage.

CLASHING ROCKS

Open-source software, Web 2.0 technologies, hardware-as-a-service, software-as-a-service, and thin client architectures represent five alternative technology delivery models that are receiving a lot of attention. If prudently deployed, they can save companies a great deal of money, as long as the corporate culture accepts them.

Open-Source Software

Instead of positioning open-source software (OSS) as competition with proprietary software, we should see it as an augmentation to it; in fact, within a few years it will begin to replace significant stacks of proprietary software as it lives alongside persistent proprietary software. Will we see

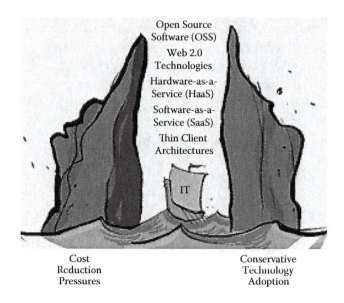

Open Source
Software (OSS)

Web 2.0
Technologies

Hardware-as-a-
Service (HaaS)

Software-as-a-
Service (SaaS)

Thin Client
Architectures

IT

Cost
Reduction
Pressures

Conservative
Technology
Adoption

FIGURE 4.4
Clashing technology rocks.

the increased adoption of open-source desktop software (to compete with MS Office) and even Linux on the desktop? Will we see the widespread adoption of open-source CRM and database applications? Many companies, especially smaller ones, will move toward holistic OSS solutions. In response to this trend, the major proprietary software vendors will reduce their prices to avert the increased adoption of open-source solutions. It remains to be seen how aggressively they fight, but they have to make some tough decisions soon because OSS solutions are growing in functionality and therefore popularity.

Companies are looking at StarOffice and OpenOffice, among other OSS applications. SugarCRM is an interesting alternative to proprietary CRM applications. MySQL is an alternative database management platform. Many companies are already running Linux and Apache, and therefore have some experience with, and commitment to, open-source software. Companies should derive cost and performance metrics from this experience and develop business cases for open-source alternatives.

Can you save money with OSS? There is no question that significant money can be saved by deploying open-source software. There are deployment strategies that optimize the role OSS can play. There are open-source applications of all kinds that should be piloted to determine their cost–benefit.

Does OSS challenge the status quo? It does, and then some. Many CIOs and CTOs cannot bear to forsake Microsoft Office for OpenOffice or even Symphony, let alone Google Docs. There's major culture shock at work here, shock that some technology managers and executives package as fear and loathing. The data, however, suggest that the adoption of OSS is growing, especially in Europe. The upward trend began before the financial world came to an end. The legitimization of open-source software coupled with pressure to reduce costs will tilt adoption toward more, not less, open-source software.

Web 2.0 Technologies

Web 2.0 technologies are fast, cheap, and flexible. They are inclusive. They are transparent. R&D crowdsourcing, for example, can reduce R&D expenses by hundreds of thousands if not millions of dollars. The problem is with conservative corporate cultures that worry about listing the problems that are challenging them. "Why in God's name," a CIO recently said to me, "would we actually *publish* our problems, or our research agenda?" Similarly, "Why would we create blogs or wikis for competitors to observe?" In some recent research we noted that the adoption of Web 2.0 technologies is surrounded with concerns about support, scalability, and security.* Some companies have actually banned the use of social networks and other social media.† Others are monitoring their employees to determine if social media are interfering with work and undermining productivity. Other companies are aggressively looking for ways to exploit Web 2.0 technologies.

Web 2.0 technologies represent opportunities to change processes, save money, and challenge the status quo. Wikis can replace course management systems for training. Blogs can augment customer service and new product development. RSS filters can be used to help customers find the information they need. Mashups can accelerate application development and deliver new functionality quickly and cheaply. Fast and cheap is the Web 2.0 mantra. So how will this play out?

---

* See Stephen J. Andriole, *Web 2.0 in the Enterprise: From Hype to Impact*, Cutter Consortium, July 1, 2008.

† San Murugesan, *To Ban or Not to Ban: Social Networks Stir Workplace Issues*, Cutter Consortium, March 11, 2008.

Hardware-as-a-Service

Do we need data centers? Probably, but we can rent the hardware from any number of vendors. Even better: we can hire a managed service provider to run our data centers (with rented hardware and software). We will assume behind-the-curtain interoperability via the industry's improving standardization of interfaces and the formalization of SOA and EDA, but do we really care how integration and interoperability happen? The price:performance ratios of hardware are improving dramatically every year. Companies such as Amazon, EMC, Yahoo, and others are renting servers for pennies. Other hardware can be leased, begging the question: do you need to own (and support) hardware?

Many CIOs and CTOs feel strongly about hardware ownership and support (just as many feel strongly about software ownership and support; see below). If there's no history of renting or leasing hardware there may be resistance to the approach. But when it comes time to replace 1,000 PCs or 100 servers, will companies buy/install/support or just rent? (Even more radical: will companies launch pilots to eventually remove all PC costs? The bring-your-computer-to-work [and we'll connect you to the network] model is beginning to get traction in large companies. How many years longer will companies buy/rent PCs for their employees?)

Software-as-a-Service

As I've said over and over again, software-as-a-service is an alternative delivery model that permits companies to avoid the care and feeding of multiple software applications. SaaS is not just for e-mail, workflow, or CRM. Enterprise resource planning applications can be rented as easily as business intelligence applications. Some providers are renting open-source applications that are even cheaper than paying by the drink for proprietary applications. Functionality will drive decision making, not brand names. Sure, Siebel CRM sounds better than SugarCRM, but do you care about the name? (How many people laughed at the name "Google" when it first appeared?)

Not only is SaaS almost always cheaper, it's also faster. Implementation time is usually almost 50% shorter than the conventional in-house installation of large proprietary enterprise applications.* So what's not to like about SaaS? Well, there's the security issue, again. There's the fear that once a company goes down the SaaS road, there's no retreating to in-house installation and support. There's some question about vendor stability and capitalization, although with the major players entering the SaaS market these fears are unjustified.

Is SaaS a viable trend or a flash in the pan? The Wall Street analysts who cover software companies think that SaaS is the future. Microsoft, Oracle, IBM, and HP are all hosting software; they have also licensed third-party providers to host their software. When the major vendors begin to participate in a new delivery model, even if they haven't led its adoption, then the entire industry will move in the same direction. Even ultraconservative CIOs and CTOs appreciate the validity that Microsoft, Oracle, IBM, and HP bring to a new technology or delivery model.

Who wins the argument? The technologists who want to control technology assets or the managers who want to reduce costs, improve speed, and step away from the technology business over time?

Thin Client Architectures

Why do we need fat clients running bloatware? Thin clients provide the ability to completely avoid break-and-fix headaches, expensive software upgrades, and even virus penetration.

The segmentation of users makes sense. Some users will remain power users and require as much computational power in as small a footprint as the industry provides, but some require much less resident power. Most users do not require a great deal of computational power or local storage on their personal devices. The vast majority of users can perform more than adequately on thin clients with no local processing and no storage. These browser machines connect to servers that host the applications, data, and storage that users need to perform their jobs. These machines are reliable, cheap, secure, and light. Software distribution disappears in this architecture, as does the need for machine-by-machine virus protection. Break-and-fix requirements

---

* Rebecca Wettemann, vice president of Nucleus Research, compares deployment times for customer relationship management (CRM) applications: 1 to 3 months for a SaaS application, 18 months for an in-house licensed application. (http://blog.ezasset.com)

also disappear: given their low unit cost, when the machines break they are simply replaced.

So what's the problem with cheap, secure, light, and bulletproof? Hard to tell, because the major risk, network availability, is all but gone. Some still argue for local storage, although the more local storage the greater the security risk. It would be surprising if thin client architecture did not grow dramatically over the next few years.

Open-source software, Web 2.0 technologies, hardware-as-a-service, software-as-a-service, and thin client architecture represent five alternative technologies and technology delivery models that can save us all a lot of money. But, as suggested above, there's a tension between these technologies and delivery models and the criteria that determine the pace of technology adoption. Put another way, there are biases against change and against anything that's not tried and true.

Caution to the Rocks

Technology adoption turns on context. When a company is in trouble, it tries lots of things to regain its competitive edge. When an industry sector is in trouble, it reinvents itself. But when trouble fails to distinguish among companies, sectors, or even continents, then drastic steps are necessary to right the ship. These days we find ourselves in a major economic crisis. Some companies are fighting themselves as they try to adapt to falling revenue and shrinking profits. Technology acquisition, deployment, and support are in the crosshairs of many companies. With technology budgets ranging anywhere from 2% to 10% of gross revenue, companies are understandably looking for ways to reduce technology costs in spite of the cultural idiosyncrasies that sometimes keep them from helping themselves.

We are on the cusp of a major shift in the delivery of information technology. Although we can expect start-ups to lead the way, mid-sized companies have also discovered the joys of technology independence. Even large enterprises are looking to alternative technologies and technology delivery models to save them money. In spite of cultural idiosyncrasies, biases against change, and any other kind of resistance to change we can think of, the big five technologies/delivery models will be adopted faster than their traditional counterparts were adopted. The time for comfortable slow deliberation is over.

These are just some of the trends and decisions that require attention. There are others worth noting. Cloud computing, the integration of many technologies and services into a plug-and-play environment, is emerging as an overarching technology delivery model. Companies can plug into the cloud for a variety of services that they can add (or delete) over time. It remains to be seen if cloud computing replaces much of what we now define as outsourcing and on-demand computing, but it's very safe to say that delivery models such as cloud computing will become increasingly popular, if only as pilots, as a means to cost-effective technology delivery.

In addition to the five technologies and delivery models discussed here are technologies that have already proven themselves as cost managers. High on the list are virtualization and voice-over-IP (VoIP). In fact, it's possible to rank-order technologies according to their likely cost impact and then pilot them one by one against a set of performance metrics that speak to cost and service.

The global economic crisis and its impact on just about every technology in the world are altering technology adoption "best practices." The clashing rocks of cost reduction and conservative technology adoption will yield cost reduction. Companies have no choice but to tilt toward cost management as they struggle with their unwillingness to move too far too fast. The interesting aspect of this inevitability is that technologies and technology delivery models that may have required a decade to settle in may well only take a year or two to yield significant dividends. This, in turn, will stimulate the maturation of these technologies and delivery models which will trigger even more changes and cost management opportunities. Put another way, no one has a vested interest in wasting this crisis.

The changes in outsourcing that the current economic crisis and new technology delivery models are triggering will persist over time, forever altering the due diligence around all flavors of outsourcing. Although many of these trends were already in play before 2008, the economic crisis will accelerate their exploitation in ways we've yet to fully comprehend. Arguably, there's a sourcing sea change occurring as we speak. In fact, we see the beginning of the change in small and medium-sized businesses (SMBs) that see no need to do much in-house technology at all. Inasmuch as SMBs do not have constraints anchored in complicated sourcing histories, they are free to aggressively exploit new sourcing strategies. Large enterprises always need a big push to change (anything). The economic crisis will push them toward new sourcing strategies in spite of their biases, cultures, and histories. Those who champion these strategies and the delivery models they embed can only cheer, however quietly, for the crisis that has become their friend.

WHY CROWDSOURCING MAKES SENSE

There's no reason to believe we know everything. Because we don't. I'm disgusted with the not-invented-here syndrome and even angrier about companies that really believe the competition is slow, stupid, and lazy. Because we're so good, and so smart, they're so bad. We dress better, too. The fact is that most companies stumble along a path to prosperity over which they have relatively little control. Of course companies need to make stuff or provide services that people want to buy. They also need to innovate enough to keep their brands in play. But when all's said and done, companies need to keep learning, from whomever they can. Technologists are no different. In fact, they need to learn more stuff faster than their counterparts in the kitty litter business. How can the learning net be cast as wide as possible? Who controls these things? We do.

Given that training budgets are just about gone these days, what's the learning strategy? Given that very few companies are hiring "nice to have" professionals on a whim (the way they did five years ago) there's a need for a strategy around problem-solving beyond your in-house gurus. One idea that comes to mind is crowdsourcing. For those who have not yet discovered the joys of crowdsourcing, let's explore why extending your brain to the web makes intellectual and financial sense.

Let's talk some more about crowdsourcing. Crowdsourcing assumes that there's brainpower on the web that can be leveraged on to your problems in some creative cost-effective ways. The cost-effective part is especially important these days. Crowdsourcing is an alternative technology acquisition model whose costs can be closely managed. In fact, business cases can be used to define crowdsourcing opportunities. For example, if a $100 ROI is necessary for a project to be successful, then crowdsourcing fees can be set accordingly. This pricing model places control in the hands of the companies that post the problems, and set the fees, and protects them from the project scope creep that always results in "adjustments" to the budget.

Other crowdsourcing projects are more process driven. Brand management, new product effectiveness, customer service, and even personal reputation management are also crowdsourcing targets. Here the outcome is not a specific problem solution but information, opinion, and insight valuable to marketers, product developers, and customer service representatives, insight that can be interpreted as positive or negative sentiment.

So what are some of the options? First, there are the venerable Innocentive and NineSigma sites: www.innocentive.com and www.ninesigma.com. These sites let you post tough problems for smart people on the web to solve. Like hired guns, they work for fees. If they don't solve the problem, they don't get paid. They're therefore motivated. The companies that post problems only pay for success. If your company invests in research and development, it's time to go to the web for help. Why in the world would you not at least pilot R&D crowdsourcing?

What else can the crowd do for you? There are all kinds of problems that the crowd can help you solve and information it can help you gather and interpret. IdeaScale (www.ideascale.com), for example, can help you organize feedback from the crowd regarding old and new products, concepts, and service, among other areas. Ideascale organizes the process on your behalf and interprets the feedback.

In fact, there are lots of vendors that help you listen to the crowd, such as Radian6, Umbria, BuzzMetrics, and ListenLogic (www.listenlogic.com). These companies, especially ListenLogic, facilitate crowdsourcing with business intelligence. New ideas about products can also be vetted through Cambrian House (www.cambrianhouse.com), along with other sites designed to stimulate discussions around innovation, process improvement, and even talent management. They've also developed a crowdsourcing engine that can be used for a variety of applications.

You don't have to go into the web for ideas. If you're paranoid about strangers, you can tap to the expertise of relative strangers, such as your employee population. Companies like Imaginatik (www.imaginatik.com) can help you leverage the intelligence of all of your employees regardless of their location or job function. This approach essentially distributes and manages the digital suggestion box.

What's the point? We're not that smart and could use some help from time to time to solve tough problems. There's a continuum of familiarity that defines comfort for many companies. "Relative strangers" who work for the company, but have never met, form one crowd, whereas "perfect strangers" who live and work on the web, form another crowd. Some companies experiment with internal crowdsourcing. Although this can be effective, it's a little contradictory or at least suboptimal, because crowdsourcing, by definition, is most effective with large crowds. Nevertheless, internal crowdsourcing is a good place to start.

Some years back there was a lot of discussion about the "free-agent nation," where individual contributors would rent themselves for specific tasks. They charged an hourly rate (in most cases) to solve discrete well-bounded problems posted by individuals or corporations. Crowdsourcing is an extension of this process but involves proactive problem posting by the companies looking (anywhere) for help. Crowdsourcing brings problems directly to the crowd, to twenty-first-century "free agents."

Companies that already rely heavily upon part-time, so-called "1099" employees should love the crowdsourcing model because it's conceptually very similar to the idea of employing professionals by the task. It's also similar to on-demand problem solving, because demand defines opportunities (and compensation). Crowdsourcing is project-driven outsourcing that in these tough economic times makes a lot of sense, even if you think you know it all. Give it a try.

IT'S A DONE DEAL

We tend to talk a lot about things long before we do them. We talk and talk and talk. Then we talk some more. We subscribe to professional talkers such as Gartner, Forrester, Cutter, and IDC, among countless other sources of brilliance. We talked endlessly about eBusiness, supply chain management, business intelligence, and digital security, and then did them all.

I also write a hell of a lot about all this. I want all of you to talk about what I write. OMG, is all this really that complicated? Can we predict what we'll do after we're finished talking? Better still, can we predict what we'll do without all the talking (and writing)? Yes we can. So here's where we're all going (whether you like it or not).

We'll all end up in the cloud. I realize that we're going to talk obsessively about when it's ready, what it can and cannot actually do, how secure it is, how well it scales, and on and on and on. But we will all end up in the cloud to some extent or another. We're already there. We're renting software. Nearly everyone has at least their heads in the cloud. We're also renting hardware, less so than software, but renting nonetheless. Even fewer of us have subscribed to the "platform-as-a-service" opportunity, but we will.

Why am I so sure about this? Because of the combinatorial effect of multiple decision drivers such as: the need to manage costs, the growing fear CFOs have about big CAPEX technology projects, the need to provision capabilities fast, the inability of many companies to police themselves with practical governance, the endless search for TCO and ROI, the lack of expertise about new architectures and technologies (especially Web 2.0 technologies and service, and event-driven architectures), the need to optimize the centralization/decentralization conundrum, and the need to escape the corporate politics that surround every single technology investment, among other simple and complex technology acquisition, deployment, and management drivers. Not to mention the core competency argument: you know, the one that asks over and over again, "Are you sure you need to be in the technology business?" Regardless of when you date the inevitability of the cloud, we can now stop talking about it and just fly into it, if only gradually, although purposefully.

We'll completely ditch computing and communications infrastructure. Does anyone really care about e-mail? Sure it's a killer communications app, but it's also the quintessential commodity. Why are you paying Microsoft (or some other vendor) huge amounts of money to enable your communications, workflow, and collaboration processes? Isn't there another way to get there? All of those who predicted the full commoditization of computing and communications infrastructure were right on the money. I love to watch the reaction of people when they learn they have 250 GB of storage on gmail for free (versus the standard 50 MB or 100 MB "allotment" that many IT departments "grant" their users). We already have multiple partners for our communications infrastructure. All that's left are the boxes, and they can be rented for pennies a day. Come on, you know it's only a matter of time. Like a month or two. When will you start the pilot?

We'll reorganize everything. Technology will not cyclically report to the CFO or the CEO. You know what I'm talking about. Every few years, when technology migrates from cost center to profit center status, CIOs alternatively report to their CEOs (who want strategic results) and their CFOs (who want to reduce costs). Part of the reason why we migrate so often is because we still house operational and strategic technology under the same roof. Why have we done this? Over the years it made perfect sense because the real difference between operational and strategic technology was negligible or, put another way, because the operational technology tail wagged the strategic technology dog.

But that was then; this is now. The objectives, acquisition, deployment, and support best practices of strategic technology are now fundamentally different from the ones that deliver operational technology. For decades we begged the businesses to get more involved in the requirements discovery and modeling process. Well, they're here, and they want to control requirements, the prioritization of business technology projects, performance metrics, and even the technology acquisition process. They're also willing to fund strategic projects. Operational technology teams should not live in the same house as strategic business technologists. The latter team is all about business results, not cost savings no matter what. Reliability, security, and scalability are assumed in the infrastructure. Strategic technology is about customers, suppliers, up-selling, service, cross-selling, marketing, sales, and innovation. Strategic technologists should live with the business stakeholders. They should report to their bosses (and the enterprise CEO). They should link with the operational technologists only on architectural and support issues.

We'll lose weight. How many years have we been talking about thin clients? How many words have been sacrificed in the name of thin client computing, thin client architectures, and network computers? It was well over a decade ago that Larry Ellison appeared on the *Oprah Winfrey Show* to talk about thin clients. (Not bad for a guy who's not too fond of cloud computing.) We were always undermined by the availability, security, and speed of our networks, nothing else (except perhaps the grumblings of the Flat Earth Society and the Luddites). Well, it's 2011 and we're just about there. We are nearly network-ubiquitous and nearly fast enough. "Nearly" means a couple of years in case you're wondering, not five or ten. By the way, the thin client surge is not just about browser-based netbooks with no local processing or storage. It's about smart phones. How many users really need laptops, desktops, or even thin clients versus smart phones? We'll get there. It's only a matter of a year or two before companies de-PC their employees.

We'll replace ourselves. Here's the deal. The skills necessary to enable the inevitable trends described here are often the ones in short supply. We'll have to deepen our skill sets or find professionals who can help us with the directions in which we're moving. Displacement is inevitable. Let's stop talking (and writing) and start doing.

ENTERPRISE SOFTWARE: NOW YOU SEE IT—NOW YOU DON'T

Oracle, SAP, and Microsoft really need to rethink their fee structures. On-demand applications, open-source software, and the growing repository of web-based components will threaten existing software delivery models to the breaking point. Do the vendors really understand this or are they in denial?

Let's dig deeper. Let me tell them what I really think and what they should do to become part of the solution rather than part of the problem. Oracle, SAP, and Microsoft are of course on the list of usual suspects; however, there are many other enterprise software vendors, including IBM and CA, that also need to pay attention to the trends about to flatten them.

First and foremost, enterprise software vendors, acknowledge that the world has changed and will continue to change regardless of what you think should happen or what you want to happen. You are no longer controlling this playing field. You have two broad choices: dig your heels in and try to squeeze the last pennies out of antiquated software licensing models or embrace the changes so enthusiastically that you begin to lead the software delivery revolution, which you have, incredibly, begun to cede to upstarts such as Salesforce.com. I realize that this is tough, like asking John McCain to admit that Iraq was incredibly stupid, expensive, and pointless, or Barack Obama to say out loud that he rejected public campaign financing because he can raise so much more money outside the system than inside (and that John McCain would have done exactly the same thing if the fundraising abilities were reversed). Enterprise software vendors need to admit change—not failure—but they need to do it proactively, aggressively, cooperatively, and, yes, enthusiastically.

We are at the end of the CAPEX technology era. Deep investments in hardware and software are coming to an end. Listen up software vendors: a ton of CIOs and CTOs are past weary about maintenance and upgrade fees. Every year more and more technology buyers would like to expense their technology investments annually rather than spread their cost over many years. We are at the end of the proprietary software life cycle. CIOs know it, CTOs know it, and even CFOs know it. You all need to go somewhere to work all this out. Here's what a summit should yield:

- A commitment to rapidly evolve your business model away from CAPEX-driven enterprise software licensing to alternative delivery models.
- Invest in software-as-a-service, not on a token basis but in a leadership capacity, directly challenging the business models of the SaaS vendors: why should they own this delivery model? Have you lost your minds? Why let them own this space? Are you still not sure the world is changing? Do you still think off-shore drilling will solve our energy problems?
- Proactively work with your clients to offer them migration paths to hosted, pay-by-the-drink delivery models. I realize that this is heresy, but wouldn't you rather lead them somewhere than chase them later?
- Build templates for migrating from internally hosted applications to externally hosted ones. These prepackaged configuration management tools would go a long way toward building your credibility and keeping your customers happy (and just plain keeping them).
- Embrace open-source software. Sure, it's the anti-Christ but it's also the future. We all know that there will actually be proprietary open-source flavors but the interoperability of these hybrids will be vastly superior to what we have today. You all need to think about becoming the Red Hats of your industry.
- Publish all of the APIs you have and support them. Make sure that they're clean and secure and update them on a regular basis. Give them away free with a smile, and keep them coming.
- Redefine your relationship with your clients as partners, not adversaries. If you think you're welcome in most enterprises then you probably thought U.S. troops would be greeted as liberators by the Iraqis. As you know all too well (perhaps after a few necessary glasses of wine), many of your clients really hate the vise you keep them in. They do not see you as a partner or a friend; they see you as someone trying to squeeze as many dollars as possible from their shrinking technology budgets. You really need to turn this around and fast, lest you lose more and more of your long-suffering clients to alternative software delivery models.

The real challenge is the reinvention of your business while you simultaneously cannibalize the business model that made you billions of dollars over the past few decades. I know, I know, it's hard to do these kinds of things, but, trust me, the clock is ticking. If you fiddle too much longer, you will trip into a free fall that will cost you billions over the next few decades.

WHAT THE EARLY TWENTY-FIRST CENTURY (IN RUINS) IS TEACHING US ABOUT TECHNOLOGY DELIVERY

"Everything's negotiable" is a phrase we hear a lot these days. It applies to buying a car, a home, or even a vacation. It really applies to technology services. We interviewed 20 CIOs and CTOs about how to optimize their vendor relationships and heard some interesting, if not provocative, things. Here's what we learned.*

Renegotiations

The CIOs and CTOs, to a person, reported that they've recently renegotiated many of their vendor contracts, even if they were happy with the contract and the performance of the vendor. The times require all of them to squeeze their vendors in search of better terms, improved performance, and, of course, cost savings. The vendors, it was reported, were cooperative, recognizing that they have little choice in these economic times but to accommodate their clients.

The drill was a simple one. Vendors were invited in to review the terms of existing contracts and the performance to date. The vendors were told well in advance that they would have to defend the terms and performance of existing contracts. The clients expected to have services improved for less money. Yes, this is a perfect reflection of the times. We were not surprised to learn that the CIOs and CTOs assumed that they could get more for less. We were surprised to learn that the vendors apparently assumed the same thing (although obviously they did not enjoy the conversations that resulted in their providing more services for less money). Contract revisions followed the meetings.

The CIOs and CTOs also built in multiple off-ramps and performance evaluations into the revised contracts. This effectively institutionalizes

---

* We conducted phone interviews with the CIOs and CTOs over a three-month period of time.

continuous contract reviews, a trend that can be explained almost completely by the economic crisis in which we all find ourselves.

Subsidies

The CIOs and CTOs, under extraordinary budget pressure, all reported that they expected their vendors to contribute more than just less money for negotiated services. They also expected them to subsidize their innovation efforts. The interviewees reported that they described their innovation agendas to their vendors and invited them to participate directly in the pursuit of innovation-focused projects.

They reported that nearly all of the vendors were willing to subsidize innovation-focused projects with money, products, and staff. The vendors appropriately expected that if a specific pilot project were successful and a corporate rollout anticipated, that the subsidizing vendor would share in the proceeds of the rollout. Some of the CIOs and CTOs use ratios to determine the range of acceptable subsidies. For example, as discussed above, if a CIO is spending $5,000,000 with a vendor they might expect a subsidy of 10%, or $500,000. The CIOs and CTOs report that 3% to 5% is more realistic. The vendors build the subsidy budget from cash, equipment, and staff to remove the sting of an all-cash subsidy.

Many CIOs and CTOs reported that the subsidy game must be played carefully. Over time vendors will build the expected subsidy into their initial umbrella contract, building the subsidy into their cost proposals and operating budgets. Understanding this, sophisticated CIOs and CTOs actually segment their budget negotiations to directly include subsidies. The vendors, especially in this economic climate, are only too happy to help their clients invest in initiatives that could increase their long-term revenue. Isn't that the ultimate carrot?

Technology Trends Assessments

Vendors love to talk about all of the good things they're doing for their clients and about all of the cool technology they have in the pipeline. Unfortunately, these discussions are almost always with sales, marketing, or business development professionals. Our CIOs and CTOs reported that they'd prefer not to speak with sales/marketing/business development professionals, but would rather speak to those actually creating the technology-driven product enhancements: the senior technologists creating the next-generation functionality that the CIOs and CTOs need to understand to make their technology plans.

Nearly all of the CIOs and CTOs found their time with sales/marketing/business development people a waste of time. Worse, many found the experience annoying and time consuming, with no useful outcome. Some of the vendors pushed back on requests to visit their rocket scientists but eventually granted access. When smart people meet with smart people good things usually happen (not that sales, marketing, or business development people are not smart, just motivated differently).

Alternative Delivery Models

All of the CIOs and CTOs reported that they are extremely interested in piloting the alternative technology delivery models that are all the rage, all of the X-as-a-service models. They're also interested in whole new ideas such as ceasing the acquisition, deployment, and support of PCs for employees and off-loading all education, training, and certifications to employees expected to pay for professional development out of their own pockets.

CIOs and CTOs expect their vendors to help them strategize about these alternatives. They also expect them to subsidize pilots. There's some suspicion that enlisting vendors to help them shift or decrease revenue is ill-advised, but most of the vendors, especially the large software vendors, fully understand the need to change the way they deliver and support their products. That said, it might be a tough sell to Dell to enlist them to subsidize pilots that result in companies buying fewer machines. But a thin client pilot is right up their alley. The migration from internally hosted enterprise applications to an on-demand SaaS delivery model should be fully participatory including all of the stakeholders.

The challenge to vendors is timing. CIOs and CTOs expect them to help them exploit vendor products and services with extended or whole new services, but on the other hand they also expect them to help their clients radically rethink their technology acquisition, deployment, and support strategies. It's this latter task that drives a wedge between vendors and clients, because the vendors perceive that radical changes in strategy may result in radically decreased spending. Our CIOs and CTOs explain this as a conundrum but at the end of the day do not believe that vendors can be trusted with anything beyond their own vested financial interests. Although the actual timing of a major change is always in question (and negotiable), our CIOs and CTOs expect their vendors to assist their plans to migrate from one delivery model to another.

This section on advanced vendor management was distilled from interviews with CIOs and CTOs in the toughest economic trenches we've seen in decades. What are the takeaways?

- All existing vendor contracts should be renegotiated. This can be awkward, but it's opportunistic and likely to yield cost savings even from your best vendors. Continuous contract review in the form of off-ramps and frequently scheduled performance reviews is the way to proceed for the foreseeable future.
- Subsidies should be expected and programmed: explicit discussions about subsidy expectations should be conducted. Defining ratios is a best practice, but it should be done carefully. The best approach is to segment budget negotiations so the cost of services is negotiated separately from subsidy budgets.
- Technology trends analyses should be a cooperative effort between vendors and their clients. Clients have a real need to understand the technology trajectories of all of their vendors. The best source of information about these trajectories is not the sales, marketing, or business development teams of your vendors. Always talk to the rocket scientists actually developing the technology you might be able to exploit.
- Alternative delivery models represent opportunities to make money and save money. Clients should pilot the models against a set of specific performance metrics. Vendors should participate in and subsidize these pilots. If vendors are unwilling to participate clients should find vendors who will assist them especially with the migration from older to newer technology delivery models.

These takeaways suggest what the final exam will look like. So go negotiate with your vendors and prepare to be harshly graded. These are tough times for everyone.

FINAL THOUGHTS ABOUT SOURCING

It's time to pull all of the internal plugs you can find. The sourcing landscape is totally different from what it was just five years ago. The whole technology delivery model has morphed into a by-the-drink, expense-driven suite of processes that we can all exploit as long as we alter our perspectives about control, standardization, agility, and cost management. The industry has given us alternative delivery models we can use to solve some tough business technology problems and to reorganize our acquisition, deployment, and support processes. It's your job to deepen your sourcing and vendor management competencies and to reassess your core competencies to determine if you need to remain in the technology business.

5

Organic Transformation

OVER AND OVER AGAIN AND AGAIN

I'm growing tired of solving the same old problems over and over again. You should be too. I realize that all of the consultants out there want me to keep quiet about this inasmuch as they make tons of money selling the same old solutions to the same old clients, but our inability to permanently kill very solvable problems is hurting the credibility and effectiveness of our profession. We cannot get out of our own way on so many issues, and it's not just the technology professionals I'm indicting here: there are just as many business professionals who continue to misunderstand and mismanage the business technology relationship. So let's indict everyone: we know what to do, but struggle endlessly about how to do IT. Here's what to do.

First and foremost, position people, processes, organizations, and corporate culture as the primary levers for change. Sure, technology is important, but the real leverage lies in what you do on the organic side. IT's all about the people and the organizations that surround them. If you fix the problems there you'll fix the problems everywhere.

PEOPLE

Profiling is a term made popular after 9/11. Remember? It's time to profile everyone at the company, including yourself. Who are the good ones? The bad ones? The smart ones? The stupid ones? Make the list. Live by it.

Strongly consider going to the dark side when all else fails. Manipulation, ass-kissing, and other tried-and-true techniques should be adopted and perfected. The world is strange and getting stranger. People make it so. You must stop the insanity.

You need to conduct a skills gap analysis immediately to determine the gap between the knowledge and skills that you have and the knowledge and skills you will need to start your business or re-engineer your current business technology organization. This is a tough love mission: you will have to eliminate some friends, relatives, and otherwise unproductive legacy people. You need business technology strategists who understand business and technology trends and the overall enterprise business technology architecture; you do not need professionals whose expertise lies in managing network latency.

Candor is an interesting thing. It frees us on the one hand, but it also constrains us. So it is with the people in our technology lives. Sometimes we love them; sometimes we hate them. Sometimes they perform well; sometimes they perform poorly. How candid are we about the technology professionals we rely upon so much? How candid are we about the executive teams who depend on them and direct their efforts?

PROCESSES

Map every process you can find. Business processes and the models they define are the lifeblood of all companies. The problem is that they usually make no sense. So set aside a bunch of buckets and fill them with good, bad, and ugly processes. Then go to work on the good ones.

GOVERNANCE

When experienced consultants walk into an organization the first thing they try to assess is the control structure that defines the company. We're all familiar with the venerable "command and control" power structure; some of us are just as familiar with collaborative management structures. Matrix management was very popular a few decades ago and today everyone's confused about the impact that Web 2.0 tools will have on collaboration, decision making, and, ultimately, control. The reason why consultants—and everyone—are so sensitive to control structures is that the distribution and specificity of power relationships inside all organizations determine what gets done.

It's amazing how many organizations cannot describe their governance structures: because they don't exist. I need to repeat this observation: many companies do not have implicit or explicit technology governance structures. How could this be true? Note that there are many companies that have elaborate governance structures that work well. But the number of companies that kick their technology decisions down the road or let the technology flowers bloom anywhere and everywhere is astonishingly high. The message here is as clear as it gets: explicitly codify a governance policy and supporting implementation and support structure that deals directly, consistently, and clearly with the acquisition, deployment, and support of hardware, software, and services. Distribute power to the senior business and technology management teams. Communicate the roles and responsibilities to the whole company, consistently and often. The senior business leadership of the company must champion the governance policy and structure.

Let's be real clear about the role that governance plays and its importance to the success of the business technology mission. If there is no (or if there is weak) governance, then the company will suboptimize its business technology investments. If there's no governance at all, the suboptimization will be enormous, which results in overspending, poor service, and religious warfare among the technology deliverers and customers, among other problems. In fact, poor, and especially no, technology governance can threaten a company's survival. Extreme? Not at all. Some companies spend hundreds of millions and even billions of dollars on technology every year. Suboptimizing by 30% to 50% will wreak havoc with every company's bottom line.

Finally, we have to point the finger at the senior management teams that allow governance to fall through the cracks of corporate administration. Ignoring the governance challenge or addressing it poorly is their responsibility. Not the board of directors, the investors, the vendors, or anyone else connected with technology. Governance is the business of CEOs, COOs, CFOs, CIOs, and CTOs. The buck stops there. Hail to all of these chiefs as long as they get the job done. (By the way, good governance speaks directly to technology rationalization, sourcing innovation, and management best practices, the rest of the "basic" areas.)

The traditional way to think about governance revolved around centralization and decentralization with decision rights distributed across the stakeholders. In the old days, way, way back in the "glass house" days, everything was centralized under the command of a technology czar. As time progressed, however, centralization yielded to decentralization. The czars countered with standardization believing that even if the lines of business had some control as long as they controlled the technology standards they were still essentially in control. The centralization/decentralization/standardization game persisted until the Internet arrived, when control was challenged by technology "consumers" (who no longer perceived themselves as "end users").

Since the mid-1990s the governance pendulum has swung wildly. In the mid- to late 1990s, technology was considered strategic. After the dot-com crash in 2000 the pendulum swung back to operational control. It stayed that way until 2003 when technology budgets began to increase. The pendulum swung from operational to strategic again where governance was shared between the enterprise CIO and the business unit CIOs (if the structure recognized BU CIOs) or just the business unit directors. We stayed this course until the world melted down again in 2008 and the governance pendulum swung back again. This time it swung all the way back to total budget lockdown where governance was centralized in the hands of a few, or just one, the CFO.

During all this pendulum swinging, something changed. Almost as though it were clandestinely taking advantage of the budgetary distractions, technology freed itself from the control of both enterprise and business unit professionals. It escaped from all of the arguments that had it swinging back and forth for all those decades. In fact, it rendered the "control" word moot.

So what exactly happened? Technology commoditized, consumerized, and left the building. It also finalized the dependency business has on the reliability, scalability, reach, and security of its digital technology. Put another, much simpler, way, business cannot turn without information technology. It simply cannot exist without IT.

Commoditization has pushed prices down and performance up. Industry consolidation has fueled standardized hardware and software architectures. It's now possible to pay less and less for more and more capacity.

Consumerization spread control to everyone. Digital technology innovation used to occur inside corporate firewalls, but now the longest technology line is at the Apple store in the mall. Social media came into corporations through windows left open by Gen X and especially Gen Y. So what does all this mean for governance? The short story is that all of the old notions of governance will be challenged by the technology commoditization, consumerization, and delivery.

Figure 5.1 describes a very different governance roadmap. Note first the distinctions among operational technology, strategic technology, and innovation technology. Next note the range of stakeholders. There are the usual suspects, all of the corporate and business unit clients, but there's also a new cast of characters, including vendors, providers, partners, and even "the cloud."

How can this be? Here's why the range of governance and the number of governance stakeholders is dramatically different today (and tomorrow), and why the whole notion of control will yield to what we might call "participatory" or "shared" control. All of these technologies are already governed in a shared way. The fact is that if a profit-generating business unit wants a strategic application to improve its product or service development process, it will get it. It will either work with enterprise IT or go around IT.

	Operational Technology	Strategic Technology	Innovation Technology
All Corporate Clients			
Business Unit Clients			
Hardware & Software Vendors			
Service Providers			
Corporate Partners			
The Crowd			

FIGURE 5.1
The new governance matrix.

The new governance stakeholders include all corporate clients, business unit clients, vendors, partners, and even the cloud. Corporate clients are the mainstay of clients. They use technology to communicate, collaborate, solve problems, make decisions, retrieve data, and all of the other operational tasks that define their professional existence. Business unit clients see technology as a conduit to their customers, suppliers, alliance partners, and colleagues in the cloud.

Vendors, service providers, partners, and colleagues in the cloud are also governance stakeholders. Vendors and service providers are special stakeholders because their products and services offer de facto governance. Companies that outsource huge amounts of their operational infrastructures essentially outsource their technology standards and the governance around those standards. Although the standards themselves can be broad (a break from the past's interpretation of "standards") they nonetheless define what the hardware, software, and service offerings will be. Environments that outsource lots of technology and technology services share governance with their providers. Similarly, suppliers and other partners frequently require specific technology-based transaction processing, which also results in shared governance. The last category of stakeholder, the crowd, is one of the most dramatic challenges to corporate governance. Why is the crowd part of the governance team? How are governance power and decision rights shared among the stakeholders? The crowd, as well as many companies, is the source of a variety of "extensions" to everyone's technology capabilities. The best examples of this are the application programming interfaces (APIs) published by companies and individuals, APIs that make it possible for clients and their providers to extend the functionality of the applications quickly and cheaply. But are all APIs OK to use? Governance must extend well beyond the corporate firewall to include policies and protocols for the use of externally developed, yet tremendously powerful, APIs and other software widgets that can be used to enhance functionality.

In addition to APIs and widgets, the crowd can also provide expertise. We are moving quickly toward a "free agent" approach to selected corporate problem solving. What if you need to develop a dashboard, a process, a chemical, or a drug? Might you turn to the cloud? What if you moved your help desk to the cloud and paid the specialists when they solved problems and your clients were satisfied? Who governs all this?

Figure 5.1 presents the new governance control matrix. There are several aspects that are important to note in what will become a sustained governance model for us to consider and implement. Figure 5.1 also distributes decision rights. The number of checks in each matrix indicates the distribution of rights across the stakeholders and three technology areas. Note that everyone has some rights in every cell in the matrix. This is an important departure from the harsh governance models of the past. Note also that points are assigned to each stakeholder. Each cell has a total of 15 points.

We could debate the number of points each stakeholder receives, but that's not the main issue. The allocation of points means that governance is shared among stakeholders. Gone are the days when governance meant that it was the enterprise way or the highway, or when business units plotted coups to topple the storm troopers in corporate.

Put another way, governance can be seen as negotiable. The governance principles are codified (as they should always be); however, the principles are by definition collaborative not hierarchical, interpretive rather than rigid, and negotiable rather than nonnegotiable.

This is a departure from our past governance practices. It acknowledges the expansion of the number of governance stakeholders, the commoditization of technology, consumerization, and the increased practice of outsourcing operational and, increasingly, strategic technology. It is impossible to ignore these trends and continue to see governance through a twentieth-century lens. Instead, the argument here is to explicitly acknowledge the trends and to adjust governance to accommodate the stakeholders who all see their objectives a little differently. Sharing governance authority is a natural result of how the field itself is changing. It's impossible for IT executives to expect to exercise the kind of control they exercised in the 1980s or 1990s. The new business technology alignment opportunity is through shared governance.

Commoditization, consumerization, and alternative technology delivery models have changed forever the way governance is defined and implemented. The number of stakeholders has increased dramatically and the role of technology has expanded into three distinct categories (operational, strategic, and innovation). The governance mission is evolving toward a shared participatory approach that recognizes the roles that all of the stakeholders play as they acquire, deploy, and support technology. Figure 5.2 suggests that there are six stakeholder and three technology categories. Governance should acknowledge the role that each plays in the optimization of the business technology relationship.

	Operational Technology	Strategic Technology	Innovation Technology
Allocation of Governance Points	5: Enterprise 3: BUs 3: Vendors 3: Providers 1: Partners 0: The Crowd	2: Enterprise 5: BUs 2: Vendors 2: Providers 2: Partners 2: The Crowd	2: Enterprise 4: BUs 3: Vendors 3: Providers 1: Partners 2: The Crowd

FIGURE 5.2
Shared governance.

RATIONALIZATION

Technology must be rationalized. This includes the infrastructure, applications, and communications networks. Way too many companies fail to inventory their technology assets. They have little total cost of ownership (TCO) data on these assets and the assets are not linked to current requirements or strategic objectives. Hell, many companies don't even know why they still have many of their applications (although they still support them).

Technology rationalization requires all technology to pass through a business value filter as well as filters that assess technology's TCO and return on investment (ROI). Ideally, there's a business technology strategy that requires technology projects to be aligned with business objectives. Technology trends should also be used to rationalize technology. The objective of technology rationalization is the identification of the right technology, where "right" means cost effective, agile, secure, scalable, and aligned (with business objectives). Rationalization is also continuous: what worked last year may not work next year. TCO and ROI data should be continuously collected. Like all of the basics, rationalization is a disciplined, data-driven process. Or at least it should be.

Rationalization is a basic best practice. Yet many companies avoid it because it's usually, if not always, political. Give me a break: technology is not personal. It's business. Technology gets old, breaks, and becomes obsolete. It should be objectively and brutally assessed every single year. If you can't get it done, then hire some vendors to do the dirty work. (Using vendors to define and enforce governance is also a tried and true best practice, if only for the weak.)

Let's also not forget that as we outsource more and more technology rationalization requires revisiting every single outsourcing agreement:

rationalization is technological and financial. Bad technology deals just like bad technology should be decommissioned.

SOURCING

How deep is your vendor management expertise? Probably not very deep. In my experience, most companies do not fully understand the mechanics of service-level agreements (SLAs), SLA management, performance metrics, shared risk contracting, or vendor-subsidized pilots. Nor do they have a sourcing strategy that systematically do SWOT analysis of alternative sourcing models, such as in-sourcing, cosourcing, and extreme outsourcing as they all involve the new delivery models.

Corporate cultures, aging technology professionals, and other biases and predispositions conspire to keep sourcing strategies in the twentieth century. These days the world's abuzz about software-as-a-service (SaaS), hardware-as-a-service (HaaS), communications-as-a-service (CaaS), and cloud computing. What's the strategy here? How are corporate core competencies serviced by alternative sourcing models?

Sourcing basics require that companies first determine their core competencies, then assess their technology acquisition, deployment, and support track record, then identify sourcing models that acknowledge both the competencies and the track record, and select the model that makes the most sense. The due diligence around alternative sourcing models is everyone's knitting—what everyone who vets alternative sourcing models routinely conducts. Both the business and technology organizations should participate in the development, selection, and implementation of alternative sourcing models. If the desire to explore alternative sourcing models doesn't come from within then look outside for the motivation and skill you need. In other words, you can get back to basics with or without your own people.

INNOVATION

When they tell you to think outside the box, I was once warned, don't take the bait: they don't really mean it and if you venture too far from the ranch they'll permanently close the gate behind you. Innovation is a stepchild in most companies, even the ones that describe themselves as creative. Note how many companies turn to the outside for innovation, even to crowdsourcing as a methodology for stimulating new ideas. What's the problem here? First, lip service is not commitment. Innovation, even in tough times, is everyone's responsibility. Incentives should be created to interest even the passive but potentially brilliant employees. The net should be cast wide: innovation can come from multiple sources. A plan should be developed and funded. Professionals should manage the innovation process. How hard is all this? Not very hard at all, especially because employees generally enjoy thinking creatively (more than sitting at help desks or writing stupid marketing slogans). Innovation is a process, not a series of discrete steps. There are also tried and true tools that can stimulate innovation, tools such as business process modeling (BPM) that can in this instance help you create new and improve old processes. Crowdsourcing is another approach. Innovation networks, inside and outside the firewall, should be created. It's essential to develop and execute an overall innovation strategy. Microsoft and IBM do most of it in-house; Cisco does a lot of it through acquisitions. What's your innovation strategy? Does it work? How do you measure it? Innovation is everyone's job. If you have to return to basics then you've already missed too many innovation opportunities.

MANAGEMENT "BEST PRACTICES"

It's hard to know where to begin here. The number of management best practices ignored by many companies is astounding. Requirements validation, project management, program management, business case development, TCO and ROI analyses, SWOT analyses, and a whole host of other methods, tools, and techniques used to optimize technology acquisition, deployment, support, and performance are often ignored by the largest "most successful" companies. Project management offices (PMOs) come and go. Business cases are developed and ignored. Due diligence is a foreign concept to many acquisition teams. No one seems to know how to kill a failing project. What the hell is going on? In spite of all the discussions, conferences, white papers, monographs, short courses, and books on "running IT like a business," relatively few companies actually do. No, let's be really candid: hardly any do.

Why is it so hard to be disciplined? I was once told by a CIO of a Fortune 50 company that the $250,000,000 that could be saved annually if applications were rationalized wasn't enough because the rationalization exercise would "upset" too many people. (Yes, you read the number correctly, and, yes, you heard correctly: "upset".) Adherence to management best practices is, like governance, political. Keeping everyone happy, avoiding tough conversations, pandering, refusing to make objective assessments of talent, among a ton of other conflict-avoidance practices, make it impossible to achieve anything but incremental improvement and even that is restricted by just how dense your political culture is.

Basics? The basics are what many of us would tell our interns or undergraduates about what to do, what not to do, and how to, um, run IT like a business. The cruel reality, of course, is that not that many businesses are run like a business. Discipline is hard to define, much harder to implement, and even harder to sustain. I'm not sure how this all breaks down but I can tell you that after years and years (actually decades) in the trenches we've hardly left the twentieth century, we're still arguing over obvious things, and we still decide what to do and what not to do based on our personal relationships and personal financial vested interests, not on what the industry tells us are best practices or what the data tell us is best for our companies. Put another way, your journey back to basics may be harder than you think.

INTERNAL CONSULTING—GO FOR IT

One last thing. Ideally, you should transform your best technology professionals into McKinsey consultants. We all know really good business technology consultants. We also know really bad ones, or "evil consultants" as I like to describe them. Good consultants have certain skills that make them valuable to their clients, skills that are "hard" and "soft." Yes, good consulting is not just about being glib and fashionable. Good consultants know a great deal about business *and* technology and, most important, where the two optimally meet. Evil consultants have problems with facts and objectivity. Good consultants want their clients to succeed.

Just about everyone hires consultants from time to time: strategic consultants, tactical consultants, and even consultants who "coach" managers and executives. We hire consultants for a variety of reasons.

If we're completely honest with ourselves, we hire consultants to really help us solve complex problems, to help us define and prioritize problems, and to say things to management that we'd rather not say ourselves. Does that make some consultants shills? Of course, and everyone knows the role when it appears on the corporate stage. Shills are not necessarily "evil consultants." Good consultants can shill good ideas and powerful business cases while keeping their professional integrity intact.

Let's focus here on good consultants and the skills that make their work so valuable. This report focuses on how to grow internal consultants by examining the internal consulting process and the skills necessary to become effective internal consultants. The subtext suggests that we invest in awareness and skills training in the internal consulting area. Much of the necessary knowledge and skills are hard to find in many technology professionals who are terrific at diagnosing and fixing technical problems but often lack the knowledge and skills to nurture the increasingly important business technology relationship.

We look at some distinctions among internal and external consulting, the consulting process, and the knowledge and skills necessary to become effective internal consultants. Along the way we just have to discuss corporate culture, organization, and politics, inasmuch as they affect so many things at every company. Then we summarize things into an action plan.

INTERNAL VERSUS EXTERNAL CONSULTANTS

Business problem solving is complicated by many variables. There are perennial uncertainties about the external environment, there are inconsistencies within internal environments; and there are specific knowledge and skills that can, when leveraged properly, accelerate problem solving. Some of these skills are substantive and some are stylistic. Some are much more about form than content. Problem solving requires an array of knowledge and skills that are themselves highly variable within companies and individuals. Some companies are smarter than they are facile or glib. Some are more glib than knowledgeable.

Can you train people to be complex problem solvers? There is a variety of educational and training resources available to companies that want to deepen the domain expertise of their employees. There are programs that address behavioral and related "soft" skills as well. In fact, "consulting" training programs are numerous. But there's a gap between generic consulting programs and programs that focus on consulting knowledge and skills leveraged within companies, on internal consulting. Programs that focus on the knowledge, skills, and behaviors necessary for effective internal consulting (the consulting that occurs within companies eager to improve their position in the marketplace) are hard to find.

Internal consultants are very different from external consultants. First, for better or worse (!), they exist within an existing and semipermanent organization with its own distinct culture and political style. This alone distinguishes internal from external consulting. For some, this is both good and bad: good in the sense that they know company policies, procedures, biases, and quirks, and bad in the sense that they know where too many bodies are buried. Some find it hard to deal with people they've dealt with for many years, especially if "dealing" means listening, collaborating, and acquiescing. But herein lies opportunity. For those business technology professionals who have both the capacity and will to deepen their knowledge and skills, effective internal consulting can dramatically improve the business technology relationship in many companies.

Second, the internal consultant must endure the consequences of his or her own success or failure. Unlike the external consultant, who gets to leave a company when a project concludes, the internal consultant works within the company's organization and culture sometimes for years or even decades. This changes the way consultants behave, as consultants, in their companies and requires a somewhat different set of skills to succeed. Taking the long view of relationships is challenging and sometimes individuals don't have the capacity to invest in internal relationships for the long haul, although investing is an advantage that internal consultants have over their external counterparts (who are always on the outside no matter how friendly they become with their clients).

Third, internal consulting differs from external consulting because the rewards are fundamentally different. External consultants, especially in the larger consultancies, are often on sales quotas: they sell or they go. Consultancies need to keep as few people as possible on the bench. They need not only to keep their consultants working but they also need to charge increasingly higher hourly rates to feed their margin appetites. Internal consultants are motivated by different things ranging from credibility and prestige to long-term career success directly aided by their ability to solve tough complex problems. Financial rewards are the universal motivator, but they're not the only motivation for internal consultants who often have deep personal and professional roots in the organizations they serve.

Motivational differences between internal and external consulting are huge. Internal consultants with long-term career aspirations in their companies behave differently from their external colleagues who are often motivated by short-term financial rewards. Let's turn to the process and skills that enable effective internal consulting.

The purpose of this chapter is to raise awareness of the importance of internal consulting as a path to improved business technology alignment and optimization, and to describe the knowledge and skills necessary for effective internal consulting. It ends with a look at how to grow internal consultants in your companies. The takeaway is that if we could develop and deploy effective internal consultants we could significantly improve the application of technology to business problems. This is the working premise of this chapter.

Figure 5.3 summarizes the steps in the consulting process and the consulting knowledge and skills that we expect good internal consultants to master. These knowledge and skills areas, along with a company's organizational structure, culture, and politics determine the likelihood of internal consulting success.

FIGURE 5.3

The internal consulting process, knowledge, and skills.

THE CONSULTING PROCESS: IDENTIFYING
MEANINGFUL PROBLEMS

The consulting process has many interrelated steps. Good consultants understand the sequence of events that define the overall process as well as the interdependencies among the events. Perhaps what good consultants do best is find meaningful problems to solve. The identification of meaningful problems is part art and part science. The key is to identify problems that matter to influential managers and executives. Although this is not to say that good internal consults should only focus on problems with political cachet, it is to suggest clearly that effective internal consultants select problems that have achievable solutions that matter to the people who define and implement corporate strategy, who are responsible for profit and loss, and who own operational excellence. Where are the clues?

Everywhere, but especially in promises that management makes to their investors and shareholders. Listen and read: there are clues all over the place. One way to think about problems that managers and executives take seriously is to segment them into those that—when solved—save money and those that make money, or, put another way, those who address business pain and business pleasure. Look at your company's mission statement, its strategy, and (if it's a public company) its latest investor presentation. Be careful with extremely abstract corporate strategies, however. Sometimes they are purely political documents, not roadmaps to profitable growth. But those strategies that have detailed plans, initiatives, and projects can be extensively mined for high potential problems/solutions. Finally, there's no substitute for ongoing conversations with key managers and executives, the real keepers of strategic and tactical priorities, and the owners of power, influence, and budgets.

Business pain and pleasure come in several flavors, as Figure 5.4 suggests. The key is to identify problems and solutions that make someone heroic, and we're not talking here about the internal consultant. Instead, good consultants know how to make their internal clients heroes. Good consultants also keep semiformal records of problems and possible solutions, as suggested in Figure 5.5. In addition, there are dimensions of meaningfulness that good consultants understand very well. These dimensions are

Business Pain	Business Pleasure
• Cost Reduction	• Revenue Generation
• Headcount Reduction	• Customer Satisfaction & Retention
• Cost Management	• Up-Selling & Cross-Selling
• Overhead Cost Reduction	• Organic Growth
• Other Cost Reduction...	• Competitive Advantage
	• Profit...
• Improved Business Response & Control	
• Improved Management Effectiveness	
• Employee Productivity/Effectiveness	
• Improved Supplier Relations	
• Organizational Awareness...	

FIGURE 5.4
Business pain and pleasure.

• The Business Pain Matrix – Who Owns It?   • The Business Pleasure Matrix – Who Owns It?

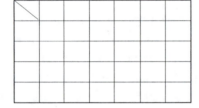
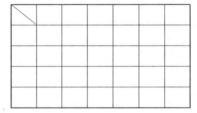

FIGURE 5.5
Pain and pleasure matrices.

sometimes brutally candid as you can see in Figure 5.6. Good consultants know full well what influences what in their companies.

Ultimately, problems have to be objectively and politically important, and they must have practical solutions. "Important" means important to influential individuals within your organization and to the company: saving money (reducing business pain) is important to executives, investors, and shareholders. So is making money (achieving pleasure). Internal consultants have a distinct advantage over external consultants in the identification of meaningful problems because internal consultants live among the problems. They are privy to the problems de jour and the changing political winds that make some problems more "valuable" than others.

Dimensions of a "Meaningful" Problem
- It's Hard
- It's Old
- It's Solvable
- It's Tied to Growth (Pleasure)
- It's Tied to Cost Reduction (Pain)
- It's Tied to Personal Bonuses
- There's Competitor Interest
- It's Tied to Wall Street
- It's Tied to Customers
- It's Important to a Boss

FIGURE 5.6
Dimensions of meaningfulness.

THE CONSULTING PROCESS: ASSESSING THE APPETITE FOR SOLUTIONS

It's important to determine how welcome solutions will be before pursuing meaningful problems. Confused? Not all problems have the right sponsors, and beyond the usual discussions about "stakeholder management" (which we have later) there are issues about sponsorship that should be identified and managed. Some of the steps necessary to assess the true appetite for solutions appear in Figure 5.7. Conversations with the right stakeholders (soon to be heroes) are critical to success. But make sure that the conversations are initially informal yet direct. All of us know that the real decisions are made before the meeting occurs. Identify the stakeholders and talk with them about the problems you want to solve and the approach you're likely to take. Do they care? Does the organization "need" a solution, or has the problem been around for years?

Outcome "what-ifs" are useful for framing stakeholder discussions. Mapping the what-ifs around problems can be very helpful to everyone:

Testing the Appetite
- Conversations with the Right Stakeholders
- Outcome What-Ifs
- Value/Cost/Risk Simulations
- Project Test Drives

FIGURE 5.7
Appetite assessment.

if the problem vanished what impact would its disappearance have on the organization in terms of pain and pleasure? What if the problem were segmented? How would that affect problem solving and the company? What if we tabled the problem until additional resources were available?

Value/cost/risk simulations are notional at this point in the process. Are there sufficient value and manageable cost and risk to justify undertaking a project to solve the problem? How does the problem "feel"? Can you simulate a problem-solving process, a real project, and can you simulate the outcome? Can you simulate the greatest threats and their impact? Can you at least conceptually simulate how cost and risk can be reduced?

Conversations, outcome what-ifs, and value/cost/risk simulations are all intended to determine a problem's value. Problems that have great value should be attacked; those with relatively little value should be tabled. Internal consultants, unlike external ones, must be extremely careful here. Credibility is a continuing issue for the internal consultant. Selecting problems that really don't matter undermines the internal consultant's credibility.

Also make sure not to get confused by the objective value of problems: there is no correlation between solutions that are important and those that are important to influential managers and executives. It's a lot like politics: politicians select problems they think can help them increase their personal power and get them re-elected, not problems that genuinely help people if the impact of the solutions might have a negative effect on their careers. Is this too cynical a view? Well, as I write this only 11% of Americans believe that their elected representatives in the U.S. House of Representatives or Senate solve the right problems. It's not all that different in companies (or other countries). Of course, the best problems or solutions are those that help personal careers and contribute to the performance of the company. Lock on to these valuable problems.

THE CONSULTING PROCESS: DETERMINING LIKELY COSTS AND RISKS

Smart consultants avoid problems with high costs and unmanageable risks. Once the expected value is understood, consultants turn to the cost and risk assessments in Figure 5.8. The skill here is an assessment of the mix of value, cost, and risk as Figure 5.9 suggests. Good consultants

What's the Cost?	What's the Risk?
• Dollars	• People
• People	• Technology
• Technology	• Organizational
• Time	• Implementation
• Opportunity	• Other?
• Distraction	
• Other?	

FIGURE 5.8
Cost/risk assessment.

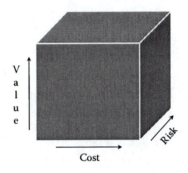

FIGURE 5.9
Value/cost/risk assessment.

understand acceptable value/cost/risk ratios and nominate problems that have "popular" and effective solutions.

Good consultants think about problems before they shop solutions among the executive elite in their companies which, of course, is no different from what external consultants do when they conceive proposals for their clients. The difference is that internal consultants have a much better feel for the value/cost/risk ratios than external consultants, who must sometimes guess about what the "best" problems and solutions look like.

Figure 5.10 should be populated by the problems identified in the pain/pleasure matrices. Value —pleasure or pain—should be vetted through cost and risk filters. Remember that all of this is about turning the lights red, green, or yellow. Red lights obviously mean stop (and go find a friendlier problem); yellow lights mean proceed with caution. Green lights keep the process going.

Who Are the Stakeholders?	Stakeholder Profile
• Solution Stakeholders • Financial Stakeholders • Organizational Stakeholders • Corporate Stakeholders • External Stakeholders	• Communications Approach • Key Interests and Issues • Current Status—Advocate, Supporter, Neutral, Critic, Blocker... • Desired Support—High, Medium or Low • Desired Project Role (If Any) • Actions Desired (If Any) • Messages Needed • Actions and Communications...

FIGURE 5.10
Stakeholder management.

THE CONSULTING PROCESS: FINDING THE RIGHT SPONSORS

More than external consultants, internal consultants understand the importance of intracompany personal relationships. The big question here is about sponsors who are also stakeholders. This is an important distinction: sponsors are always stakeholders whereas stakeholders are not always sponsors. Sponsors who are stakeholders require different management techniques than stakeholders who aren't also sponsors.

In addition, we need to profile stakeholders the way salespersons profile their customers. Who are they? What kind of role will they play? How should they be managed? Figure 5.10 summarizes this step in the process. Remember that there are interrelationships among the stakeholders that must be managed as well, sometimes decades-long interrelationships.

Effective internal consultants are good at managing sponsors and stakeholders because they understand what each participant wants and needs. Successful consultants are able to prioritize these wants and needs in ways that please just about everyone. They do this first and foremost by subjugating their personal interests and biases in favor of their clients. Not everyone can do this; not all personalities are consultative personalities. (This is an important point which we discuss later; not everyone is suited to be an internal consultant. In fact, probably less than 25% of business technology professionals have what it takes.)

THE CONSULTING PROCESS: DEVELOPING COMPELLING BUSINESS CASES

Compelling business cases emerge from the implementation of the first four steps of the consulting process. If the lights stay green, a story can be developed to persuade sponsors and stakeholders to proceed with an actual project, the scope of which is defined in subsequent steps.

The business case forms the basis of a project plan. Note that all of these steps are intended to vet the viability of a problem-solving process. A key assumption about a business case is that it will lead to an executable project. In other words, once the case is made, everyone assumes that a project plan will emerge that has a good chance of successful implementation. The business case must speak directly to importance, business pain or pleasure, and must identify sponsors, stakeholders, and major cost and risk factors that must, in turn, be defined around their own mitigation plans.

THE CONSULTING PROCESS: REALISTICALLY DEFINING PROJECTS

One of the things that good internal and external consultants do well is avoid project death marches. They know when projects, even with approved business cases, have more chances to fail than succeed, and they run from these projects all the time. Project management has over the past 10 years or so developed a kind of cult status in the industry. Project Management Institute (PMI) certification is still considered a valuable career asset. But project management is far more than charts and timelines. There's a tremendous amount of judgment and experience that determines if a project is likely to succeed or fail. Good consultants are realistic, not optimistic. There's no place for unbridled optimism in project planning or execution. If anything, good project planners and consultants at all levels are pessimists. Management gurus aside, let's argue that projects often fail because we hope against hope, assume funding and expertise that may not exist, and fail to account for illness, laziness, and stupidity. The list goes on and on. Many years ago, before Dilbert ruled the cynical corporate world, everyone embraced

"Murphy's Laws," the simplest of which was: "Everything that can go wrong will go wrong." Plan for it because, as they say, the man or woman who sets expectations low is seldom disappointed.

THE CONSULTING PROCESS: CHUNKING

Divide-and-conquer is an old strategy. It has served military commanders well for centuries. In the twenty-first century, the strategy still makes sense. "Chunking" projects piece by piece reduces risk and permits mid-project adjustments. Regardless of how PMI-certified project managers might feel about constant dependency task management, it often makes sense. The approach is simple: treat all tasks in a critical path. Task 2 cannot begin until Task 1 is complete, and so forth and so on until all of the tasks are completed. Yes, this flies in the face of agility-driven strategies and strategies designed to attack multiple tasks simultaneously (as long as resources are available). Chunking is a conservative strategy designed to reduce risk, pure and simple. Internal consultants should be inherently more conservative than external ones. Remember, internal consultants work where they live and live where they work. There's nowhere to hide when the wheels come off.

THE CONSULTING PROCESS: EXECUTING

The only difference between an hallucination and a vision is the number of people who see it. But neither is worth much without execution. Effective consultants are good at finding meaningful problems, persuading sponsors, managing stakeholders, assessing risk, and developing compelling business cases. They're also good at execution. Note that the skills necessary to execute are different from the skills necessary to conceive, persuade, and negotiate: vision is not execution. Execution requires delegation, attention to detail, inspection, measurement, and the ability to objectively assess progress, talent, risk, and cost. Chunking and execution go hand in hand. Project staffing requires special attention to the segmentation of expertise within projects. Projects without professionals who can execute will fail.

THE CONSULTING PROCESS:
REVISITING VALUE/COST/RISK

This step is really simple: never lose sight of why the project was under-taken, its cost, the risks anticipated when the project began, or the risks encountered during the project's execution. This is a constant assessment because, as Murphy warns us, everything takes longer than it takes, and optimists are people who don't fully understand the situation. Of special importance is the value/importance assessment. Projects fall in and out of favor because of strategic turns companies make. Internal consultants have the advantage here over external ones because they can quickly stop, modify, or redirect projects. Often external consultants are constrained by a negotiated statement of work (SOW) that requires long negotiations to undo. Internal consultants can stop on a dime once the new direction is defined and sponsored by the right stakeholders although it's often politi-cally difficult to significantly redirect or kill a project that an internal con-sult has vigorously sold to management. Murphy's advice? Underpromise and overdeliver.

THE CONSULTING PROCESS: REPORTING

The form and content of project reports are determined by corporate preferences. Whatever look and feel the company prefers should define reporting styles. Some companies prefer Powerpoint briefings; some pre-fer informal discussions, and other companies prefer written reports. A project is never finished, however, until the sponsors and stakeholders have been informed about progress, problems, and what's still left to do. Touching all of the players is essential; touching them the way they prefer is assumed.

All 10 steps of the consulting process are to a great extent generic; that is, they apply to internal and external consulting. But the interpreta-tion of the tasks is significantly different depending on the internal ver-sus external perspective. Internal consultants have so many advantages over external consultants especially in the areas of problem definition, prioritization, and negotiation. At the same time, they are somewhat constrained by their long-term commitment to their companies: they

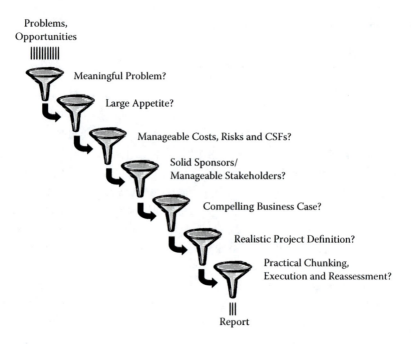

Problems,
Opportunities

Meaningful Problem?

Large Appetite?

Manageable Costs, Risks and CSFs?

Solid Sponsors/
Manageable Stakeholders?

Compelling Business Case?

Realistic Project Definition?

Practical Chunking,
Execution and Reassessment?

Report

FIGURE 5.11
The consulting process.

cannot make enemies and at times may overcompromise in their business case and project negotiations. All in all, the internal consultant is potentially much more effective than the external one, especially if he or she widens and deepens his or her business knowledge and behavioral skills. Figure 5.11 summarizes the process as a set of filters. Consistent with the above recommendations about project chunking, this is a critical path waterfall.

CONSULTING KNOWLEDGE AND SKILLS

The other side of effective internal consulting is knowledge and skills. Business and technology knowledge lie at the core wrapped in a set of skills that are often described as "soft." Let's run through the list of knowledge areas that make internal consultants effective. We then turn to the skills and behavior that enable this knowledge.

Knowledge of the Business and Functional Business Areas

This is the area where internal consultants have a tremendous advantage over external ones. How many times have you hired external consultants who then proceeded to ask a series of very basic questions about your company. Valuable time is lost when OJT (on the job training) is required. Internal consultants know the industry their companies are in as well as the companies themselves. As already suggested, they know the policies, procedures, biases, templates, and where the bodies are buried. This makes them tremendously valuable to their colleagues.

So what else should they know? Here's a short list of the essentials:

- *Basic Business Knowledge*: Knowledge about management, finance, accounting, marketing, and all of the areas that enable the acquisition and application of more specific industry and company knowledge.
- *Collaboration:* Knowledge about the interconnected marketplace and internetworked companies; knowledge about what happens inside and outside companies: the collaborative mindset.
- *Customization and Personalization:* Knowledge about mass personalization, behavioral models to correlate online and offline behaviors, wireless personalization, and personal and professional CRM, among other related areas.
- *Supply Chain Management:* Knowledge that includes supply chain concepts, models, and tools. Integrated supply chain management (by the vertical industry in question) would be a central focus here along with the technologies that enable supply chain management as well as SCM standards, technologies (such as exchanges), and some of the leading SCM platforms.
- *Project and Program Management:* Knowledge about project management processes, methods, and tools as well as program management processes, methods, and tools. The range of areas would include several varieties of business technology project management and several varieties of program management, including business technology acquisition strategies, managing outsourcing and service-level agreements, among others.
- *Partner Management:* Knowledge that includes approaches, methods, and tools for managing relationships with distributors, resellers, service providers, and so on.

- *Regulatory Trends:* Knowledge about regulations and regulatory trends in specific industries and hit lists for tracking legislation that could have a significant impact on business policies, processes, and procedures.
- *Manufacturing:* Knowledge, as appropriate, about your industry's manufacturing processes and technologies.
- *Distribution:* Knowledge about the industry's distribution practices.
- *Service:* Knowledge about the industry's approach to customer service.
- *Mission and Values:* Knowledge about your company's core mission and the values to which it subscribes.
- *Competitor Intelligence:* Knowledge about specific competitors, including information about their sales, marketing, profitability, strategy, and so on.
- *Policies, Procedures, and Discipline:* Knowledge about the way your company operates, how it's organized, how it makes decisions, how it rewards and punishes people, how it deals with suppliers, customers, and partners, what it likes and dislikes, and insights into its "personality."
- *Relationships:* Knowledge about the relationships the company has with its suppliers, customers, partners, benefit providers, and so on.

Knowledge of Technology

Good business technology internal consultants understand the technology industry and the technology business. In addition to the basics, they understand the acquisition, deployment, and support processes, and the technologies that power business models and processes. The ideal range of technology knowledge includes:

- *Basic Technology Knowledge:* Knowledge about hardware, software, and services; the structure of the technology industry; the major technology players; conventional and emerging technologies, especially web-based technologies.
- *Applications Architectures:* Knowledge that looks at how mainframe (single tier), client–server (two tier), and Internet/intranet (3 tier → *n* tier) applications have changed and what are the trade-offs among the architectures (defined around flexibility, scalability, reliability, etc.); knowledge about service-oriented architectures (SOA), event-driven architectures (EDA), and related business technologies.

- *Messaging and Workflow:* Knowledge that examines the platforms that support all varieties of communication and how communications technology enables communication and transactions among employees, customers, and suppliers inside and outside the corporate firewall.
- *Database Management and Analysis:* Knowledge that positions data, information, knowledge, and content of all varieties (static, dynamic, text, video, etc.) and how it can be managed for alternative purposes, as well as data, knowledge, and content management platforms, next-generation database management applications (especially object-oriented and multimedia DBMSs).
- *Integration and Interoperability:* Knowledge that describes the technical requirements for making disparate incompatible applications, standards, data, platforms, and architectures communicate with one another, focusing on enterprise applications integration (EAI) and Internet applications integration (IAI), wrapper/glue technologies including XML and Web Services (and SOA and EDA), as well as more conventional middleware. The knowledge should focus on the need for, and objectives of, integration and interoperability, including cross-selling, up-selling, customer service, alliance building, and so on.
- *Business Technology Metrics:* Knowledge designed to introduce professionals to ROI, EVA, and TCO (and other) models for assessing business technology effectiveness. Business case development and due diligence should also be included here.
- *Security and Privacy:* Knowledge that examines the concepts, models, tools, and technologies that enable security architectures, authentication, authorization, administration, and business resumption planning. The technologies would include encryption, biometrics, PKI, and smart cards, among others.
- *Business Analytics:* Knowledge about the processes and technologies that yield insight from sales, marketing, customer service, finance, accounting, technology infrastructure, and competitor data; knowledge about the forms that analyses can take.
- *Business Technology Acquisition Strategies:* Knowledge that examines all aspects of the technology procurement and support process, including especially in-sourcing, cosourcing, and outsourcing.

- *Automation:* Knowledge about intelligent systems technology and the application of that technology to personal and professional automated transaction processing, monitoring, e-billing, and the like, including methods (neural nets, fuzzy logic, expert systems, etc.) and how these methodologies can be embedded in tools and applications.

- *Optimization:* Knowledge that looks at major technology and business processes and how they can be optimized with a variety of models, tools, and technologies as well as the need for integration, interoperability, and synchronization and how optimization becomes the nexus for productivity and profitability. Optimization concepts, models, tools, and technologies can be applied to technology performance (network optimization, for example) and business process performance (applications design and development, training, customer acquisition, etc.).

- *Business ⟷ Technology Convergence Strategy:* Industry- and company-specific knowledge that examines methods for developing and assessing business technology strategies in specific and converging vertical industries. Some of the models and methods that would be included are scenario planning, decision modeling, and alternative futures development. These methods would then be linked to major technology investment decisions around applications, communications, data, and the like. Such knowledge would help consultants understand the relationship between vertical collaborative business strategies and integrated computing and communications technology.

The business and technology knowledge areas together represent a wish list of knowledge areas that, ideally, all business technology consultants possess. Just imagine if all of these areas were mastered by a single consultant or even a team of consultants. Well, there are a number of external consultancies, including DiamondCluster International, the Boston Consulting Group, McKinsey, and others that have business + technology expertise. Because there's precedent for wide and deep expertise, let's agree that the combination of business + technology knowledge and internal consulting skills would be an incredibly powerful combination of knowledge, skills, and abilities.

Skills, Abilities, and Behavior

The friendly side of knowledge is "form," expressed as skills, abilities, and behaviors that good consultants master to solve problems. Some of the most important abilities and skills include listening, conversing, negotiating, influencing, persuading, synthesizing, writing, and presenting (along with the dark-side skills we discussed earlier).

Good consultants are terrific listeners. They understand that through "active listening" they will understand things better and build a communications relationship with their sponsors and stakeholders.

Figure 5.12 illustrates the generic communications process. The elements are well known, but rather than focus on a happy linear process we focus on what can go wrong with each element. There are all sorts of problems with senders. Some of them talk too much; some too little. Some are abrasive and obnoxious. Some tell very bad jokes. Some focus on personal issues way too much. Some are aloof and condescending. Some are unaware of how they are perceived by the receivers of their messages, perhaps the worst mistake any consultant can make. Some like to complain about everything, but especially their colleagues.

Good consultants know what they know and don't know. They know how they are perceived; in fact, they know what "box" the receiver has probably placed them in (and they understand that the box may be different for each receiver). They can see their profile in the receiver's eyes. They adapt to it; they never fight it or try to remake their image in their client's eyes.

Introspective senders, who are often good consultants, are able to shift the edges of their demeanors and personalities to blend with their receivers. It's more than checking a CRM customer file to learn if a client likes

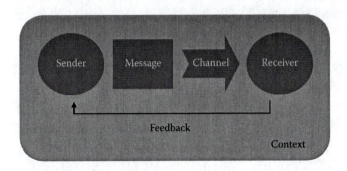

FIGURE 5.12
The communications process.

football, golf, or the ballet and then reading up on the favorite area the night before a meeting. It's an emotional intelligence (EQ) process where demeanors and personalities are modified to meld with the demeanor and personalities of clients.

There are just as many problems with messages. Some consultants spend a lot of time on form and very little on content; some messages are content-heavy but ugly. Good consultants understand that both style and substance are important but that the relative contribution of each to a message changes based on a number of factors. For example, some receivers prefer (actually demand) stylistic messages: for these receivers form is as important as (or more important than) content. Others just want the facts: they couldn't care less how pretty the form is. Most effective consultants understand that messages must have the right form and content. The real preferences are about content and form depth. Content depth refers to the length of messages and the amount of detail embedded in the message. Form depth refers to the lengths some consultants go to select the right font, graphics, and colors to communicate their message. It's actually pretty easy to profile receiver preferences: watch the feedback you get from receivers and adjust your message form/content accordingly. Hint: if you send a 300-word e-mail and get a 3-word response, there's probably too much depth in the message.

What about the channel: how the message is sent? There are lots of problems here as well, especially because we all like to (over)rely on digital communications channels such as voicemail, e-mail, and text messaging. The issue here is receiver preference. Some receivers prefer face-to-face communication, and some actually prefer after-hours voicemail. Some like to text their way through meetings and some really love long e-mail threads. Whatever the receiver prefers should influence the selection of the communication channel. Recognize, however, that not all channels are perfect, far from it, in fact. There are many consultants who worry a lot about between-the-lines interpretations of e-mail. Others believe that back and forth voicemail is not the best way to communicate. Smart consultants communicate through channels that their receivers (clients) prefer, but they also audit the impact of these channels. Sometimes, consultants add or delete channels along the way given the feedback they receive during the communications process.

Finally, there's the receiver. How many problems lie under that rock? Well, just as with senders, there are all sorts of issues, challenges, and opportunities. Senders need to profile receivers before the message form/content and channel are selected. Again, this profiling goes way beyond the kind of data profiling that exists within most CRM applications. Deep profiling identifies values, biases, quirks, and motivations. What's important to the receivers? How do they feel about quick-and-dirty versus slow-and-steady? Are they comfortable or uncomfortable with candor? Are they defensive employees who worry about making a good impression and never making mistakes, or are they inclined to take some risks, recognizing that they might sometimes fail? Are they spiritual or religious? The key is to accurately profile the receivers not just in terms of their demeanors, predispositions, personalities, and values, but also in terms of their preferences regarding the form/content/style substance of the messages and channels they prefer.

There's some feedback and context at work here as well, as Figure 5.11 suggests. The communications process is continuous. Good consultants adjust and adapt as the communications process unfolds. They are also influenced by the political, organizational, and cultural context in which communication occurs.

Related to all this is the ability to converse and persuade through negotiations. Put another way, consulting effectiveness is determined by one's ability to sell. Clearly, the ability to speak clearly and concisely, and to carry on purposeful conversations, is essential to successful consulting. The ability to persuade and negotiate is also essential inasmuch as so much of consulting involves prioritization, trade-offs, cost–benefit analyses, and resource allocation.

There are a number of negotiating styles to consider, including competitive, collaborative, compromising, accommodating, and avoidance-based. These styles all have (obvious) features and are applied at different times according to the receiver, the message, the channel, and the context.

Negotiations require preparation. The relationships among the participants must be mapped and profiled. Will existing relationships affect the negotiation? In what ways? Expected outcomes must also be listed. What does everyone expect from the negotiation? What are the expectations regarding the process? Consequences must be described. What happens if the consultant "wins"? "Loses"? What happens to the relationships after the negotiations? What about power? Who has it before, during, and after the negotiation? Who controls the resources? Finally, compromises must be identified before the actual negotiations begin. For what would the consultant settle? For what would the client settle? The key to successful negotiation is preparation.

Writing is another important skill. As many of us already know, writing is a skill that not enough professionals possess. For any number of reasons, there's less emphasis placed in the educational process on writing than there should be. But unlike many of the knowledge and skill sets required for effective internal consulting, this one can absolutely be improved through training and practice. It's a skill not wrapped up in some native ability like the personalities we inherit.

The ability to present to friends, colleagues, and even strangers is also a skill that can be improved through training and practice. Audience analysis is an acquirable skill.

All of these skills, abilities, and behaviors define an effective internal consultant. Like the list of knowledge areas, this list is formidable. Obviously, not everyone has all of the bases covered on either list. But many really good consultants from many of the above-mentioned consultancies have many of the bases covered and are able to take the business technology relationship to the next level.

The ability to synthesize business and technology knowledge and skills and abilities, all within a consulting process, is a true talent. Synthesis is an art and a discipline. It requires simultaneous top-down and bottom-up thinking. The reference early in this chapter to the ability of many technology professionals to solve technology problems is often the result of bottom-up thinking. Top-down thinking is "big picture" directed and a skill that many strategists, visionaries, and good consultants have. (The formal discipline for all this is known as "systems thinking.") This is a nontrivial skill. The ability to synthesize apparently disparate elements requires perspective, multidisciplinary knowledge, and a pragmatism that's difficult to combine. One of the steps that results from successful syntheses is modeling. There is a variety of modeling tools and techniques available to the consultant, which include:

- Cause and effect diagrams
- Systems diagrams
- Flow charts
- SWOT (strengths, weaknesses, opportunities, and threats) analysis
- Porter's five forces model
- PEST (political, economic, sociocultural, and technological) analysis
- Value chain analysis

These and other tools and techniques are often used to represent holistic thinking about solutions. They are inherently graphic and therefore facilitate understanding. Good consultants know which tool or technique makes the most sense for the right problem to communicate with the right sponsors and stakeholders.

CULTURE, ORGANIZATION, AND POLITICS

Consulting occurs in a context of sanity and insanity. We refer to this as corporate culture, political context, the ranch, or some other metaphor that communicates instability and dysfunctionality. Murphy would remind us here that all organizations are pathological: it's just a question of degree. The impact of culture and politics is seen in the organizational structure that defines the roles and responsibilities of the rats in the maze. Who reports to whom, who runs what, and who gets rewarded are the derivatives of structure, culture, and politics. Sometimes it works, from the perspective of the majority of employees, but often it fails miserably.

People exist in corporate cultures, sometimes among leaders of dubious character and capability, and within a set of rules that define just how happy or crazy the crew actually is. When we think about daily life at the ranch, we tend to think about the overall political environment in which we work. But politics is just one aspect of the overall context that influences decisions. The others include the culture of the company, the quality and character of the leadership, the financial condition of the company, and the overall financial state of the industry and the national and global economies, all as suggested in Figure 5.13.

Effective internal consultants are good at assessing the political culture of their companies. Some companies are almost completely "political": a few people make decisions based only on what they think, who they like (and dislike), and based on what's good for them personally (which may or may not be good for the company). Other companies are obsessive-compulsive about data, evidence, and analysis. In the middle are most of the companies out there, with some balance between analysis and politics.

Corporate culture is a key problem-solving driver. Is your culture adventurous? Conservative? Does your company take calculated risks? Crazy risks? Are you early or late technology adopters? Does your culture reward

FIGURE 5.13
The whole consulting context.

or punish risk takers? It's important to assess corporate culture accurately. Technology investments must sync with the culture (as well as the rest of the variables that comprise the total decision-making context). Business technology decisions in analytical cultures tend to be driven by total cost of ownership and return on investment calculations, but technology decisions in highly political cultures often have bad outcomes.

At the heart of the matter is the balance between analysis and politics or, expressed more gently, research and philosophy. For example, business technology decisions occur within a philosophical context often expressed in dicta such as, "We don't believe in off-shore outsourcing," or "We never build applications; we always buy and integrate them." These kinds of philosophical preferences drive the problem-solving (and consulting) agenda. Decisions that make the list are then approached analytically or politically, depending on the culture. Maneuvering through decision-making mazes can be challenging or rewarding depending on the size of the consultant's personal/corporate culture gap.

An important organizational issue—especially in global corporations—is the centralization/decentralization ratio of activities, functions, and responsibilities. Consulting requires an acknowledgment of the control processes at work in an organization. Consultants must assess the role that governance plays in the administration of corporate rights and privileges.

There are vast differences in the form and content of solutions in centralized versus decentralized organizations.

Many companies are schizophrenic. They oscillate between centralized and decentralized organizational structures. Some companies are transitioning from one form to another. There is a definite moving target phenomenon at work here. Consultants need to pay very special attention to the centralized/decentralized dance and make sure that their solutions align with the structure du jour. Why all the emphasis over centralization and decentralization? Because organizational structures are about governance, power, and control. If a consultant gets this wrong, he or she will pay dearly.

The role of the business relationship manager has recently become more and more important in the business technology relationship in many companies. One of the early responses to the "alignment problem" was the creation of business relationship managers responsible for bridging the gap between business problems and technology solutions. The best ones tilt toward the business even though they usually come from the technology side of the company. These ambassadors for the optimization of technology are sometimes excellent candidates for deeper consulting training. Many of them have already self-selected into the role, which requires many of the skills and abilities discussed here. Business relationship managers may represent the core consultants in your organization.

The mixture of culture, organization, and politics determines the degrees of freedom a consultant has to maneuver through a company. Good consultants avoid problems they cannot fix, such as what they perceive as deranged corporate cultures. They understand the impossibility of altering senior management teams or the resultant politics that explain how things work (or fail) in a company. Smart consultants focus on what's doable and fixable, especially in the short term.

All of this is another way of saying that internal consulting is constrained (or liberated) by the parameters of culture, politics, leadership, and organization. Consulting opportunities come and go based on these parameters. Although we don't like to think in terms of limits and constraints, reality (and Murphy) knows better. The best consultants profile not only senders and receivers but companies as well. Sometimes good consultants leave their companies for greener pastures with fewer limits and constraints. This is perhaps the hardest decision a successful internal consultant must make. Should you stay or leave?

Finally, we should acknowledge the impact that the financial state of the company has on consulting, not to mention the quality of a company's leadership. Companies losing lots of money will expect all of their consultants to present only killer business cases for company-changing or company-saving projects. Companies flush with cash will expect their consultants to think boldly about how to make even more money. Unfortunately, there's no substitute for solid leadership. Bad leaders will underexploit good consultants. Good leaders will work closely with good consultants. There's not much one can do when the idiot son-in-law takes over the company.

WHAT NEXT?

Experienced internal consultants can help your company solve complex problems. But as mentioned earlier, you probably don't have as many employees suited for internal consulting assignments as you might think. Why? Because the knowledge and skills necessary for successful internal consulting are hard to find in individual professionals: there's a reason why only a select few make partner at professional services firms. So what should you do?

Some companies have developed executive education programs to introduce the idea of the value of internal consulting. They run their high (consulting) potential employees through the program to see what shakes out in terms of interest and ability. Many of the employees decide they really don't want to be internal consultants and others just don't have the knowledge and skills to be effective internal consultants, or the ability to learn them quickly enough for them to be valuable to their companies. But some of them fall in love almost immediately. Some business relationship managers, for example, latch on to the consulting mantra as a way to increase their influence, credibility, and performance. These are natural candidates for consulting certifications.

Note that there may well be some sensitivities around who gets to go to "the program." In our experience the number of interested professionals will exceed both your capacity to train and your best judgment about who to train. More directly, there will be some members of your team who think they are absolutely qualified to become certified consultants, yet reality will screen them out of the queue. This is an opportunity to practice some consulting skills, in this case, negotiations. You will have to persuade the interested but unqualified parties that their contributions to the company are huge, even without a professional certification in internal consulting. Some of them will be unhappy with this line of reasoning; some will accept it. The best advice here is to identify the disconnects as soon as possible so any disappointment about exclusion is minimized. The fact remains that there will be some excellent professionals interested in internal consulting who for one reason or another should not be invited to become certified internal consultants.

The evaluation process should begin with an invitation to high potentials to determine their interest in, and capacity for, internal consulting. The result of the executive awareness program should be a short list of interested and capable professionals who should receive more professional training, ending with a certification in professional consulting. Ideally, the provider of the professional certification will customize the program's content to the company's industry, culture, organization, and politics.

The premise of this chapter is that there are things that professional consultants do and knowledge and skills that they have which make them effective at solving complex business problems. This knowledge and skill set can be leveraged within companies especially given the advantages that internal consultants have over external ones when it comes to industry- and company-specific expertise. The premise further states that if we select the right people we can grow effective internal consultants who will apply much of the same knowledge and skills that the best "good" consultants apply every day.

The call here is for the professionalization and certification of internal consultants. Think about how effective your very best business relationship managers would be if they were trained and certified in internal business technology consulting.

All of this is about business technology optimization. Over the years we have invested in many initiatives to improve the business technology relationship. Internal consulting is another initiative with great potential. If your organization has achieved a level of relationship success with town meetings, internal marketing, and the deployment of business relationship managers, then an investment in internal consulting should pay good dividends.

Epilogue

These are all the tricks I have. The key is to focus more on people, processes, organizations, and cultures than on technology. There are all sorts of steps you can take to bring technology to the next level of impact at your company, but these steps are organic, not digital.

Your company may be confused at first; actually, they might remain confused. But pay no mind to the inmates: you know what to do. Get the people, processes, organization, and culture right and you have a good chance of cost-effectively deploying technology. Get them wrong and there's absolutely no chance of getting IT right.

Ultimately, we should end up with a consulting mindset, the attitude that problems are definable and solvable (if certain things are true), notably governance, reasonably sane people, processes that make sense, and organizational structures that support and reward problem solving. Good consultants have great soft skills, you know, the people skills necessary to navigate through permanently troubled waters.

Focusing our energy around people, processes, organizations, and cultures—and not technology—is challenging on so many levels. We tend to solve easy problems first, and then over and over again. These days the "easy" problems are technology problems. It wasn't that many years ago that selecting a PC standard for your company was complicated. Servers crashed all the time. E-mail was spotty. This stuff all works now and acquisition, deployment, and support issues are well understood. The remaining challenge, the challenge we avoid, is organic. It's time to redouble our attention to people, processes, organizations, and cultures. If we acknowledge the importance of this foursome we can make significant progress toward optimizing our investments in digital technology. If we continue to ignore the foursome we'll remain mired in the neuroses, *non*-sense, and paranoia that describe most technology environments today. But look at IT this way. Focusing on people, processes, organizations, and cultures is more entertaining, although more frustrating, than worrying about PCs, servers, networks, or digital rights management. So thicken your skin and get to work.

Index

A

Abstractions-into-solutions, 26
Access device strategy, 27
Accountability, 29
Acquisition, innovation through, 105
AI. *See* Artificial intelligence
Alignment, 10–11
    strategic risk management and, 108
Alignment-to-partnership strategy, 36–38
Alternative delivery models, 118–119, 140–
        141. *See also* Delivery models
    governance and, 165–167
    vendors and, 157–158
Alternative technology delivery models,
        70
Analytical corporate cultures, 30–31
Analytics
    cost–benefit approaches, 86–88
    database management and, 75
App store, 53–54
Application architecture, 4
    consultant knowledge of, 186
    globalization and, 61
Application projects, saving money with,
        94
Applications, assessment of, 90
Architects, 17
Architecture, 3–4
    business technology and new models
        of governance, 52–53
    explaining to executives, 78–79
    practice areas of, 4–5
    strategic and operational technology
        and, 49–50
Artificial intelligence (AI), 27
Ass kissing, 15
Automation, consultant knowledge of, 188

B

BAs. *See* Business analysts

Best practices
    explaining technology to executives,
        79–80
    management, 170–171
Blogs, 54, 143
BPM. *See* Business process management
BRMs. *See* Business relationship managers
BTMO. *See* Business technology
        management office
BTRM. *See* Business technology
        relationship management
Budget flexibility, globalization and, 63
Budgeting
    guerilla, 98–99
    project prioritization and, 89
Business analysts (BAs), 57–59
Business analytics, consultant knowledge
        of, 187
Business and technology knowledge
        synthesis, consultants and, 188
Business applications, globalization and,
        61
Business architecture, 4
Business cases, 12–13
    development of by internal
        consultants, 181
    tough love, 116–117
Business intelligence, 27
Business knowledge, internal consultants
        and, 185–186
Business pain and pleasure, 175–176
Business performance management, 10
Business process management (BPM), 67,
        112–113
Business process modeling, 75, 170
    strategic risk assessment and, 109
Business processes, reassessment of, 89
Business relationship managers (BRMs),
        57–59, 195
Business strategy, role of IT department
        in, 81
Business technology
    degree programs for, 97